ALSO BY **THOMAS J. VOSPER**

Historic Pub Crawls Through London: Volume I
Historic Pub Crawls Through London: Volume II
Historic Pub Crawls Through England
Historic Pub Crawls Through New York

HISTORIC
PUB CRAW[L]

Through
IRELAND

HISTORIC PUB CRAWLS

Through
IRELAND

*Ten guided walks around Ireland's
iconic pubs and landmarks*

THOMAS J. VOSPER

SPHERE

SPHERE

First published in Great Britain in 2026 by Sphere

1 3 5 7 9 10 8 6 4 2

Copyright © Thomas J. Vosper 2026
Maps © David Andrassy 2026

The moral right of the author has been asserted.

All rights reserved.
No part of this publication may be reproduced, stored in a retrieval system, or transmitted, in any form, or by any means, without the prior permission in writing of the publisher, nor be otherwise circulated in any form of binding or cover other than that in which it is published and without a similar condition including this condition being imposed on the subsequent purchaser.

A CIP catalogue record for this book
is available from the British Library.

ISBN 978-1-4087-2298-5

Designed by Clare Sivell
Typeset in Minion Pro by Clare Sivell
Printed and bound in Great Britain by Clays Ltd, Elcograf S.p.A.

Papers used by Sphere are from well-managed forests
and other responsible sources.

Sphere
An imprint of
Little, Brown Book Group
Carmelite House
50 Victoria Embankment
London EC4Y 0DZ

The authorised representative
in the EEA is
Hachette Ireland
8 Castlecourt Centre, Dublin 15,
D15 XTP3, Ireland
(email: info@hbgi.ie)

An Hachette UK Company

www.hachette.co.uk
www.littlebrown.co.uk

To everyone who has joined me on pub crawls,
and everyone still to do so.

CONTENTS

Foreword ... ix
About this book ... xi
Preface ... xiii
How to use this guide ... xvii

IRELAND

Dublin South (Merrion Row to Temple Bar) ... 3
Dublin North (Glasnevin to Baggot Mile) ... 25
Galway (Latin Quarter to Eyre Square) ... 51
Limerick (People's Park to Poems) ... 71
Cork (River to Theatre) ... 93
Kinsale (Fort to The Market) ... 111
Waterford (Bridge to the Ships) ... 127
Dingle (Marina to Dick Mack's) ... 147

NORTHERN IRELAND
Belfast (City Hall to the Cellars) **163**
Derry (Peace Bridge to the Walls) **183**

IRISH LEGACY
Boston (Fenway to the Park) **201**
Boston (Revolution to Freedom) **221**

Picture credits 245
Acknowledgements 247
How to get involved 249
About the author 251

FOREWORD

The best pubs in the world are in Ireland, so it is only right that we have a historic pub crawl laid out for us to enjoy.

From beautiful city pubs in Dublin and Cork to smaller towns filled with gems like Kinsale and Dingle, there are so many opportunities to become immersed in the culture, community and heritage.

My favourite style of pub is an old, untouched one that has been around for years, even better if it's in a setting that used to be a family home, like Kennedy's in Dingle.

It's hard not to fall in love with the well-known popular spots like Dick Mack's in Dingle or O'Connell's in Galway – places that are known all around the world and still give visitors an experience both to remember and keep coming back for.

I think the most Irish experience you'll get is in an old pub in Dublin, beside a very famous graveyard, at John Kavanaghs, also known as 'The Gravediggers', where I first met Thomas in 2024. We shared a pint in the famous snug as the owner of the pub shared his family stories under the smoke-stained ceilings.

We also had a chance to visit The Palace Bar in Dublin, one of few remaining Victorian pubs in the city; a pub filled with mahogany wood & people chatting.

You'll find these spots, and many more, included in this book of pub crawls through Ireland.

Thomas has a love for pubs around the world like no other. I've enjoyed his crawls throughout London and I'm so happy he's decided to create such memorable routes here in Ireland.

You've got the right book in your hands to plan your routes, discover the amazing places that make Ireland so special, make memories with friends and family, and maybe even learn a few historic facts along the way.

Cassie Stokes
Irish travel content creator

ABOUT THIS BOOK

I've spent the last twenty years arranging pub crawls with my friends and family across London, and now share the routes and pubs on social media. This book is a tribute to the locations and pubs that I have personally visited as I have expanded my travels and explored further afield.

While every effort has been made to ensure its accuracy at the time of print, there may be subsequent name changes or, worse, a pub may cease trading.

There are always more pubs to visit and, while I try to share the most interesting places (with the best beer), each selection is planned more for the enjoyment of an entire route that covers an interesting area.

I have not made any commercial agreements to endorse one particular pub over another and sadly I miss out, or walk past, great pubs all the time – usually just to ensure the route is spaced out enough to allow those following it to sober up sufficiently between pubs.

This book has no rules and is merely a guide for you to

explore the area and the pubs within it. If you pass a pub that looks good, then pop in – you never know what you might find!

PREFACE

In James Joyce's novel *Ulysses*, its hero, Leopold Bloom, attempts to cross Dublin without passing a pub. It is an impossible challenge that could apply to almost every location on the Emerald Isle.

Throughout the island, there is always a pub nearby – on a busy road, down a country lane or as the last holdout of a centuries' old building standing defiantly against Old Father Time.

I have been arranging pub crawls for my birthday since my twenties, and what started with friends and family has become a deeper passion that has enabled me to explore even more historic drinking establishments across the world and hear the stories that make them so special.

As my social media following grew around my London routes and then England, I became emboldened by my followers' enthusiasm to explore further afield and to cover more pubs. First, thanks to a fortunate opportunity, New York City, and now I am delighted to have travelled across the island of Ireland and beyond.

When you arrive in a new town or city, the pub is often the best place to start, stop off for lunch or end a day's exploring. The staff often have amazing stories to tell, and a good team behind the bar will always make a stranger feel at home by pouring a great pint. In Ireland you will find it hard to turn down a smooth pint of stout and the cheese toastie that is usually melting behind the bar.

Some of the towns covered in this book are so small that they are rammed with pubs and not much else. However, while there are not many more sights to see, the pubs themselves are among the most special I have visited.

I decided early into my prep for this book that there is much more to the island of Ireland than borders, and for that reason I have included two amazing cities in the north.

Much has been written about Ireland's relationship with the UK, so while I won't go into much detail about that, there are times when it is important to mention it when talking about the history of an area or a pub, however difficult that might be. While researching this book I felt privileged to spend time with great people, and to walk around areas that would have been out of bounds for a Londoner just a few decades ago.

As an island with not many more than seven million inhabitants, it is remarkable that there are over one hundred million people living across the planet with Irish ancestry. Their endeavour, humour and charm have spread far and wide.

After enjoying the hospitality of the Irish across New York – a city whose Irish population is so large it would be the second largest on the island of Ireland – I planned to travel further, to include other US cities and their rich Irish heritage in this book. So, I was delighted to explore Boston and its special place in the hearts of the Irish diaspora.

My travels are enhanced by the many talented young people I meet along the way, who help me film these routes for my social media. Wherever I was during the writing of this book, so many hours have been spent laughing over a beer with new friends.

I am honoured to have had the opportunity to explore this amazing island, learn more about Irish culture, and share some of the most fascinating and memorable pubs I have ever been to.

I hope you will enjoy these routes as much as I have, get to discover the stories behind the pubs for yourself, and make as many memories and new friends as I walked away with.

The best times in life are spent with family and friends, and if you are on one of my pub crawls that's exactly what you are.

HOW TO USE THIS GUIDE

Each route starts near a train station or landmark, with walking directions and a map marked with numbers that correspond to the pubs described.

Throughout the list of directions, areas of interest, landmarks or facts are lettered and the corresponding details given in the pages that follow.

This book is designed to fit in your back pocket and be easy to carry as you explore the routes. Please don't leave it on a coffee table or bookshelf, as there are many of your own chapters to include as we support our great pubs.

Should you wish to skip any pubs, or find your own route, then full pub details are provided for you to plot your own path.

The complete routes are typically around a couple of miles long, with a total walking time of about an hour, and the gap between pubs often being five to ten minutes, allowing for sufficient fresh air and recovery to maintain the energy and thirst for the next pint.

Often the routes have a few pubs condensed into a short distance, enabling you to curate your own shorter path.

Timings are provided as a guide, to ensure you can complete the route in a day with a start time that is generally around early afternoon.

HISTORIC
PUB CRAWLS

Through
IRELAND

DUBLIN SOUTH
(Merrion Row to Temple Bar)

Heading through the very heart of Dublin city centre, the route starts at the end of the legendary Baggot Mile and passes the vast St Stephen's Green and its landmarks, before heading through the main tourist areas, over the River Liffey and ending up in Dublin's oldest pub.

It is not unheard of to catch a familiar face performing on the famed Grafton Street before entering the instantly recognisable Temple Bar.

The route includes some of my favourites, such as Toners and Mulligan's, and a mix of old-school local pubs like Grogan's and Kehoes, alongside the popular Temple Bar – at the heart of the eponymous area – and the surprising and sensitive conversion of St Mary's into the popular Church Café Bar, which is a fantastic place to catch some music and dancing.

On my day filming this route I was joined by antiques expert and pub memorabilia fanatic Ian Dowling, of *Irish Pickers* TV series fame, and some of his tales are captured here.

Start at the Merrion Hotel (D02 KF79).

1. **Toners** *1.00 p.m.*
139 Baggot Street Lower, Dublin 2

2. **O'Donoghue's Bar** *1.30 p.m.*
15 Merrion Row, D02 PF50

3. **The Dawson Lounge (open from 4 p.m. Mon–Thurs)** *2.00 p.m.*
25 Dawson Street, D02 XT59

4. **Kehoes** *2.30 p.m.*
9 Anne Street South, D02 NY88

5. **The Hairy Lemon** *3.15 p.m.*
Stephen Street Lower, Dublin 2

6. **Grogan's** *4.00 p.m.*
15 William Street South, D02 H336

7. **The Stag's Head** *4.30 p.m.*
1 Dame Court, Dublin, D02 TW84

8. **Mulligan's** *5.15 p.m.*
8 Poolbeg Street, D02 TK71

9. **The Oliver St John Gogarty** *6.00 p.m.*
2 Fleet Street, Temple Bar, Dublin 2

10. **The Temple Bar** *6.45 p.m.*
47–48 Temple Bar, D02 N725

11. **The Church Café Bar** *7.30 p.m.*
Jervis Street, North City, D01 YX64

12. **The Brazen Head** *8.30 p.m.*
20 Lower Bridge Street, D08 WC64

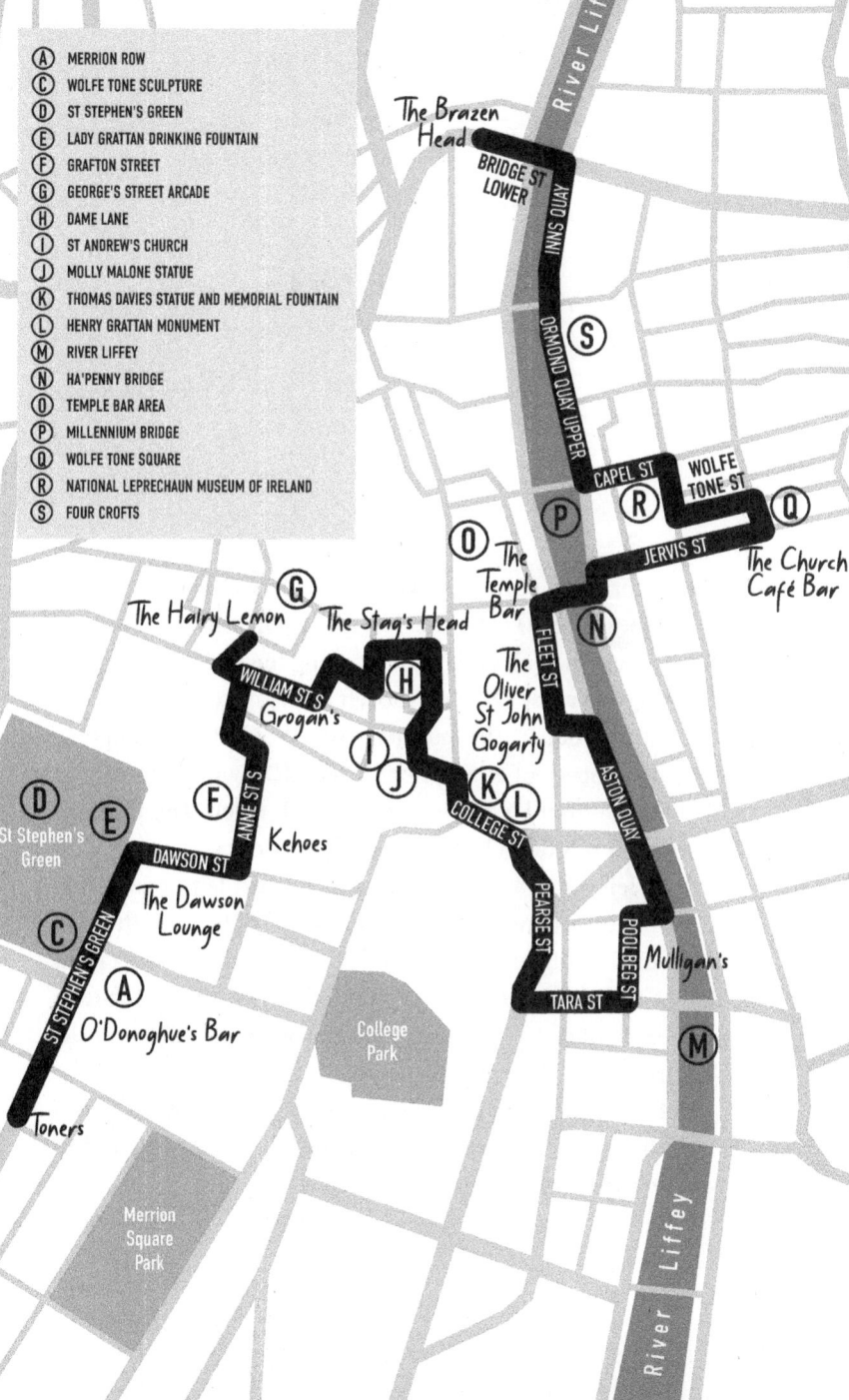

DIRECTIONS

Start at the hotel entrance **(A)** and turn left at the crossroads, where **Toners (B, 1)** is on the opposite corner of the next road along. Leave the pub and head left along the main road, where **O'Donoghue's Bar (2)** is on the left of the next block.

Continue out of the pub past the Wolfe Tone Sculpture **(C)** at the corner of St Stephen's Green **(D)**, and turn right at the Lady Grattan Drinking Fountain **(E)**, where **The Dawson Lounge (3)** is hidden behind a small red door.

Turn left out of the pub and take the next left down Anne Street South, where **Kehoes (4)** is on the right. Pass the pub and over Grafton Street **(F)**, after the road turns left, take a right along Chatham Street until a T-junction where after a left turn and a walk of just a few yards, **The Hairy Lemon (5)** is impossible to miss on the right-hand side.

Retrace your steps to the junction of William Street South and follow the road north past George's Street Arcade **(G)** to **Grogan's (6)** at the corner on the left.

Leave the pub and head along the pedestrian area, before

turning right onto Drury Street and then a quick left/right to lead up Dame Court, where **The Stag's Head (7)** is on the right at the junction.

Head out of the rear door and turn right along Dame Lane **(H)** before turning right at the end, then left towards the church **(I)**, where Molly Malone's statue **(J)** is outside. Head left up Church Lane before emerging at the main road by the statue of Thomas Davis **(K)** and turn right past the Henry Grattan Monument **(L)**, following the road left at Trinity College. Follow the road as it curves right alongside the college and past a couple of junctions before heading left past the old fire station, towards the river, where **Mulligan's (8)** is down the left turn onto Poolbeg Street.

Head past the pub and turn right at the end, before turning left at the river **(M)**, following the road. Turn left down Bedford Row a few roads before the Ha'penny Bridge **(N)**, where **The Oliver St John Gogarty (9)** is at the heart of Temple Bar **(O)**.

Continue in parallel with the river on the right before reaching **The Temple Bar (10)**. Follow the first right past the pub and cross the river on the Millennium Bridge (P) before a quick left/right to head up Swift Row past Wolfe Tone Square **(Q)**, after which it is impossible to miss **The Church Café Bar (11)**.

Turn left out of the pub and back down past the square on the left. Follow as the road curves right before turning left to the National Leprechaun Museum of Ireland **(R)** and towards the river, where a turning on the right heads past the Four Courts **(S)**. Cross the next bridge, where **The Brazen Head (12)** is on the right.

A. MERRION ROW

The elegant Georgian architecture and rich cultural history made this a popular residential area for wealthy Dubliners, and it gained a reputation as a prestigious location for the city's elite during the eighteenth century.

While its elegant townhouses have mostly been converted into commercial properties over the years, it remains indelibly linked to the culture and literature of Dublin, since the likes of Oscar Wilde were born close by.

B. 12 PUBS OF CHRISTMAS

A festive pub crawl tradition in Dublin that usually sees groups of friends visit twelve different pubs in one night. Its name comes from the fact that it usually takes place in December, with participants often seen wearing Christmas jumpers or Santa hats.

On one of my visits, I met up with 'The Guinness Guru', Daragh Curran, who knows a thing or two about the best pubs, and while I was dwarfed by his 6 foot 7 inch frame, I did a pretty good job of keeping up with the pace.

1. TONERS

This is one of my favourite pubs, and one that is often talked about the most lovingly in the city.

The building was constructed around 1818 and spent its early days as a shop – the bar is uncomfortably low, as it would have served as a grocery counter.

It was taken over by James Toner in 1921. He retained much of the original décor, including the shop's drawers, which can still be seen behind the bar.

Said to be a favourite of Irish writer W. B. Yeats, and with one of the best snugs in Dublin (check the award), the pub is like the Tardis, as it opens out into one of the largest beer gardens in the city.

I've been here before, for quiet pints, rowdy stag dos and passionate sporting occasions.

Ian Dowling of Irish Picker TV fame joined the day's crawl.

2. O'DONOGHUE'S

Legendary as the music venue that gave the Dubliners their first break, this old pub dates to 1789 when, like Toners, it operated as a grocer's shop.

It was taken over by Joe and Mary O'Donoghue shortly after it received a licence, and converted to the pub it is today.

During the 1960s folk revival it became synonymous with traditional Irish music, and often hosted impromptu sessions where Ronnie Drew's regular performances led to the forming of the much-loved Dubliners.

C. WOLFE TONE SCULPTURE

On the corner of St Stephen's Green is this statue commemorating Theobald Wolfe Tone, who was a leading figure in Irish republicanism in the late eighteenth century.

A passionate advocate for independence, he led the 1798 Irish Rebellion against British rule, which is where he was captured. Having been sentenced to death, he ended up dying in prison at the age of thirty-five.

Today's monument was unveiled in 1967 and was created through a collaboration between sculptor Edward Delaney and architect Noel Keating.

D. ST STEPHEN'S GREEN

This Victorian Park was originally a marshy common that was used for public executions and grazing livestock before it was enclosed in 1664 by the surrounding Georgian buildings.

It was not until Sir Arthur Guinness funded a redesign that it was opened to the public in 1880.

The Irish Citizen Army forces, led by Michael Mallin and Countess Markievicz, occupied the park during the 1916 Easter Rising.

Gunshots were exchanged from the makeshift trenches and the hotel buildings opposite, with bullet holes still visible on some of the stonework today.

E. LADY GRATTAN DRINKING FOUNTAIN

Crafted from polished granite, this fountain was a gift to the city from Lady Laura Grattan, who was the daughter-in-law of Irish patriot Henry Grattan.

It was erected in 1880, and provided much-needed clean water at a time when it would have been a luxury in the city. The structure would originally have included drinking cups, with horses able to drink from the basin.

It is also around this location that you might spot an amphibious jeep full of tourists dressed up as Vikings on a tour of Dublin's landmarks.

3. THE DAWSON LOUNGE

It is easy to miss Dublin's smallest pub, which is down a narrow staircase behind a tiny red door.

This underground bar occupies the basement of an 1870 building and has a capacity of just forty drinkers. The men's toilets are especially curious, as the blown-glass ceiling lets light in and people can be seen walking above.

The tiny bar is almost completely shown in this shot and you have to get here early to see it this quiet.

4. KEHOES

First licensed in 1803, this pub's Victorian character comes from a significant renovation completed at the end of the nineteenth century.

It was then that many of its notable features were installed, such as the dark stained-glass mahogany doors, a tiny snug accessible through a separate door, and the low mahogany bar that remain today.

Like many of Dublin's old pubs, it served as a shop at one time and has retained the original mahogany drawers behind the low grocery countertop. These would once have been used to store consumables like rice, tea and coffee.

It was frequented by writers and literary figures such as Patrick Kavanagh, Brendan Behan, and Flann O'Brien, gaining further fame with a mention in James Joyce's short story 'Grace', which sees a character stumble on the pub's steep stairs.

F. GRAFTON STREET

Now a busy shopping destination, this vibrant street is renowned as a destination for street performers and buskers.

Its name comes from Charles FitzRoy, the 2nd Duke of Grafton; however, it is most notable as the site of performances by the likes of up-and-coming artists such as singer-songwriter Allie Sherlock, who found fame on YouTube, and more established artists such as Damien Rice and Coldplay's Chris Martin.

5. THE HAIRY LEMON

A filming location for the 1991 film *The Commitments*, this striking corner pub was constructed around 1830 from two separate townhouses.

Throughout the nineteenth century the rooms and buildings had several commercial uses, before merging to form today's pub.

The name is inspired by a colourful character from the 1950s who was recognised by his distinctive appearance and role as the local dog catcher. His yellow hue and unkempt, stubbly features were said to resemble the bright fruit.

It was here that I caught up with German creators, the Pub Sisters, who tried to jump-scare me on arrival, despite them being the ones to spill their pints!

G. GEORGE'S STREET ARCADE

This was Ireland's first purpose-built shopping centre when it opened in 1881, making it also one of the earliest in Europe.

It was designed by British architects Lockwood & Mawson, who included striking red-brick façades and ornate ironwork.

A devastating fire destroyed much of the original market in the late nineteenth century, before it was restored and reopened just a couple of years later in 1894.

6. GROGAN'S

This no-nonsense pub is famous for its pints and cheese toasties, serving hundreds of the latter every week from behind the bar.

It has been a gathering place for artists, writers and locals since it was established in 1899, and it retains its creative roots, as the walls are adorned with a rotation of local artwork that is available to buy.

If you are here alone – as I have been – they are quick to sit you down at a table with strangers and bring your pint over to you.

During a recent trip with friends we saw a wedding party arrive unannounced and buy pints of the black stuff all round.

7. THE STAG'S HEAD

Although a pub has been present here since the 1780s, the current iteration was constructed in 1895 as a flamboyant showcase of Victorian design by local businessman George Tyson.

Much of the original interior remains, including its mosaic-tiled flooring, carved mahogany bars, stained-glass windows and ornate skylight in the rear barroom.

Given its beauty, it is not surprising that it has featured extensively in TV and film productions, with the most notable being *Educating Rita*, starring Michael Caine and Julie Walters, Albert Finney's *A Man of No Importance*, and 2014–2016 gothic horror series *Penny Dreadful*.

It's easy to miss the ornate upstairs where I sat and filmed with the Guinness Guru Daragh Curran for his YouTube channel, sharing my favourite pubs – with this one being a strong contender.

H. DAME LANE

Taking its name from the now demolished St Mary del Dam church, the lane was redeveloped as part of the Wide Streets Commission's regeneration work to turn the marshy lands into a more structured passageway.

The lane is referenced in James Joyce's *Ulysses*, as Hely's Printing Works was once located here.

I. ST ANDREW'S CHURCH

After a devastating fire demolished the original seventeenth-century church, this Gothic Revival style replacement was constructed by architect William Henry Lynn, who was well known in Belfast and across England.

It is the burial site of many notable people, such as the Lord Chancellor of Ireland, Thomas Dalton, and MP Marmaduke Coghill. Also on this site lies Esther Vanhomrigh, better known by the pseudonym 'Vanessa', a long-time lover and correspondent of writer and cleric Jonathan Swift, who famously penned *Gulliver's Travels*.

The church was deconsecrated in 1993 and served for some time as an office for the local tourist board.

J. MOLLY MALONE STATUE

Without a doubt one of Dublin's most iconic landmarks, albeit for very much the wrong reasons.

Created by sculptor Jeanne Rynhart, the bronze statue was unveiled in 1988 to celebrate legendary fish seller Molly Malone, immortalised in one of Ireland's most beloved folk songs, 'Cockles and Mussels', also known as 'In Dublin's Fair City'.

It originally stood at the bottom of Grafton Street before being relocated to its current spot on Suffolk Street in 2014.

Molly is portrayed in seventeenth-century dress, while pushing a cart laden with seafood. It is a popular opportunity for tourists. However, an unfortunate tradition emerged that led to visitors rubbing her chest for good luck. Over the years this has led to noticeable wear and discoloration of the bronze bust.

K. THOMAS DAVIS STATUE AND MEMORIAL FOUNTAIN

This monument was unveiled in 1966, on the fiftieth anniversary of the Easter Rising, to commemorate co-founder of *The Nation* newspaper, Thomas Davis, who was a leading figure in the Young Ireland movement.

L. HENRY GRATTAN MONUMENT

Directly facing Trinity College, this bronze statue was erected in 1876 to commemorate Irish politician Henry Grattan, who played a crucial role in the Constitution of 1782 that granted the Irish Parliament greater autonomy from British rule.

Originally, the monument was flanked by four ornate gas lamps adorned with carved seahorses, two of which remain today.

8. MULLIGAN'S

First licensed in 1782, it began as a shebeen – an unlicensed drinking venue. But in more recent times it has been recognised as a location for the film *My Left Foot*, which featured multiple Oscar winner Daniel Day-Lewis as writer and artist Christy Brown, who had cerebral palsy.

It took its current name when the Mulligan family moved in during 1854 and relocated to its current address.

The rear room is known as the Joyce Room, and was believed to be the setting for a scene in the story 'Counterparts', which features in James Joyce's *Dubliners*.

As well as being a popular haunt for actors and theatregoers appearing at or visiting the former Theatre Royal nearby, it was a common watering hole for journalists from the *Irish Press* and *Irish Times* offices. At one point there was a phone at the end of the bar that was jokingly referred to as 'the office phone'.

Given his time as a journalist with Hearst Newspapers, it is widely claimed that it was here that John F. Kennedy drank his first pint of Guinness in 1947.

At the rear of the bar is an antique grandfather clock that was once said to have housed firearms but now holds the ashes of American tourist Billy Brooks Carr, who considered Mulligan's his favourite pub.

First visiting the pub with his brother in 1980, they were so enamoured that they created their own version called Mama Hattie's in their home city of Humble, Texas. Billy died in 2011 and it was his final wish that his ashes be kept at Mulligan's.

It also happens to be the favourite pub of my friend Ian Dowling, whose knowledge of antiques came in handy during his stint as resident expert in the popular TV series *Irish Pickers*.

M. RIVER LIFFEY

With a name taken from the Irish 'An Life' – a reference to the plain through which it passes – the river flows for approximately 50 miles from its source in the Wicklow Mountains, onwards through County Kildare before terminating at Dublin Bay.

A key waterway since Viking times, today it is spanned by more than twenty bridges, including the cable-stayed Samuel Beckett Bridge and Mellows Bridge, the latter of which was constructed in 1764, making it the city's oldest.

N. HA'PENNY BRIDGE

Made of cast iron, this bridge was the most significant work of the Coalbrookdale Company's John Windsor and the first pedestrian-only bridge in the city when it was opened in 1816.

With around thirty thousand daily crossings it underwent significant renovations in 2001 to ensure the structure remained safe.

9. THE OLIVER ST JOHN GOGARTY

One of the city's most striking pubs, it takes its name from the multifaceted Irish figure who, as well as being known as a poet, surgeon, politician and athlete, was most likely the inspiration for James Joyce's character Buck Mulligan in his novel *Ulysses*.

Like a couple of others in the local vicinity it opens early, serves food till late and has live music on almost continuously – a proper tourist pub.

O. TEMPLE BAR (AREA)

Initially an area surrounding the residence and gardens of Sir William Temple in the early seventeenth century, it has evolved into a bustling tourist hotspot that is a popular destination for stag dos and hen parties.

Not that any of those revellers would notice that it is also home to numerous cultural institutions, such as the Irish Film Institute, Temple Bar Gallery and the Museum of Ireland.

10. THE TEMPLE BAR (PUB)

At the heart of the famous area, this pub has become an iconic symbol of Dublin's vibrant nightlife, but despite it now being Dublin's most Instagrammable pub there has been a licensed premises on this corner since around 1840.

The area around the pub has held a mixed reputation; however, during a period of regeneration in the 1990s the owners restored the building's traditional red façade, and it is now often illuminated with fairy lights, or adorned with shamrocks for St Patrick's Day and Christmas decorations in December.

Despite its touristy reputation, it provides near continual live music and oysters, with the tiny two-person snug to the right of the side entrance almost always overlooked by customers, who mistakenly identify it as a glass collection area.

Social media pals 'The Pub Sisters' gate-crashed the day and joined me in Temple Bar's liveliest pub.

P. MILLENNIUM BRIDGE

Designed by Howley Harrington Architects, with structural engineering by Price & Myers, the bridge features a slender steel truss resting on reinforced concrete haunches. The 135-foot span was prefabricated in Carlow, approximately 50 miles from Dublin, and installed in December 1999 to commemorate the approaching new millennium.

During Dublin's annual Winter Lights festival, the Millennium Bridge is illuminated in vibrant colours, earning it the nickname 'Rainbow Bridge' among locals and visitors.

Q. WOLFE TONE SQUARE

Laid out adjacent to St Mary's Church, the area is the site of a graveyard, which was deconsecrated in 1966, before being transformed into today's green space and urban plaza.

Named after the Irish revolutionary, the original graveyard is the final resting place of Lord Norbury, who died in 1831 and was known as the 'hanging judge' for his excessive use of the death penalty.

11. THE CHURCH CAFÉ BAR

My social media video of this pub exceeded three million views and it is easy to see why, as the central bar is housed within the otherwise unremarkable St Mary's Church.

The original church was consecrated in 1701, becoming Dublin's first classical parish church, and in its early years it was the location for several notable events.

Arthur Guinness, inventor of the iconic stout, married Olivia Whitmore here in 1761, before they went on to have twenty-one children together.

'Father of Irish Republicanism', Theobald Wolfe Tone, was baptised within its walls in 1763 and it also hosted Methodist Movement founder John Wesley's first Irish sermon.

After the church closed in 1986, the building was briefly used as a retail space until 1997, when a seven-year restoration project was proposed by John Keating.

Reopened in December 2005 as John M. Keating's Bar, a couple of years later it was acquired by new owners and renamed the Church Café Bar. It now attracts more than 600,000 visitors each year.

Many of the church's original features remain, such as the Renatus Harris organ and stunning stained-glass windows, under which there is live music and dancing every night.

When I was there, we managed to catch a performance by the Highkicks, a traditional Irish dancing troupe, and the video was one of my most successful ever, with millions of views online.

This spectacular bar is a stunning feature in this pub.

R. NATIONAL LEPRECHAUN MUSEUM OF IRELAND

Often a derogatory stereotype or image of the Irish, this museum was established in 2010 to share tales of leprechauns, fairies and other mythical creatures, and to champion their positive portrayal in the media.

5. FOUR COURTS

Prominently sited on Inns Quay along the river's edge, this fine example of neoclassical architecture is home to Ireland's principal courts.

Although construction began in 1786 it was not completed until 1802, with the complex housing the four original Irish courts: the Chancery, King's Bench, Exchequer and Common Pleas.

Today, the Four Courts are the Supreme Court, the Court of Appeal, the High Court and the Dublin Circuit Court.

It served as the military HQ for Commandant Ned Daly's 1st Battalion during the 1916 Easter Rising and, in 1922, amid the Irish Civil War, the Anti-Treaty forces also occupied the building.

The bombardments during the conflict led to the destruction of the Public Record Office, which resulted in the loss of nearly a thousand years' worth of historical documents.

12. THE BRAZEN HEAD

While it might proudly claim the title of Ireland's oldest pub, with its origins dating back to 1198, the current building was constructed in 1754 as a coaching inn, and Guinness World Records recognises Sean's Bar in Athlone as the oldest.

Throughout a history that goes back centuries, this popular pub has been a gathering place for notable figures in Irish history such as Robert Emmet and Michael Collins, with literary greats like James Joyce, Jonathan Swift and Brendan Behan also said to have drunk here.

Of course, today it is one of the busiest and most popular

pubs in the city and, if you have made it this far you'll have had good craic.

The first Ireland video that went viral on my social channels as we completed our twelfth pint.

DUBLIN NORTH
(Glasnevin to Baggot Mile)

Starting at the north of the city, near the graveyards, this route includes some of Dublin's most famous pubs.

While it is quite a way out of the centre, a quick bus or taxi ride leads to what is universally hailed as the best pint of Guinness in the world, served at John Kavanagh – better known as the Gravediggers.

One of the longer walking routes, this is well worth it to see a different side of Dublin, close to the football ground and then over the river and back into the more touristy spots.

Take in some iconic pubs, such as the defiant Oval Bar where scenes of the 1916 Easter Rising are all around, the modern Needle installation that towers over the city skyline and the Victorian gem that is the Palace Bar, before finishing up at the end of the Baggot Mile, which often features in Dublin's traditional '12 Pubs of Christmas' challenge.

Start at Glasnevin (D09 CF72).

1. **John Kavanagh (The Gravediggers)** *1.00 p.m.*
1 Prospect Square, D09 CF72

2. **Hedigans (The Brian Boru)** *1.30 p.m.*
5 Prospect Road, D09 PP93

3. **The Bohemian (The Boh)** *2.00 p.m.*
66 Phibsborough Road, D07 P592

4. **Parnell Heritage Pub & Grill** *3.00 p.m.*
72–74 Parnell Street, D01 ND00

5. **The Celt** *3.45 p.m.*
81 Talbot Street, D01 YK51

6. **Grand Central** *4.30 p.m.*
O'Connell Street Upper, D01 XY61

7. **The Oval Bar** *5.15 p.m.*
78 Middle Abbey Street, D01 RW24

8. **Palace Bar** *6.00 p.m.*
21 Fleet Street, D02 H950

9. **Bruxelles** *6.30 p.m.*
8 Harry Street, D02 KX36

10. **Doheny & Nesbitt** *7.15 p.m.*
5 Baggot Street Lower, D02 F866

11. **Smyth's of Haddington Road** *8.00 p.m.*
10 Haddington Road, D04 FC63

12. **Searsons** *8.30 p.m.*
42–44 Baggot Street Upper, D04 V210

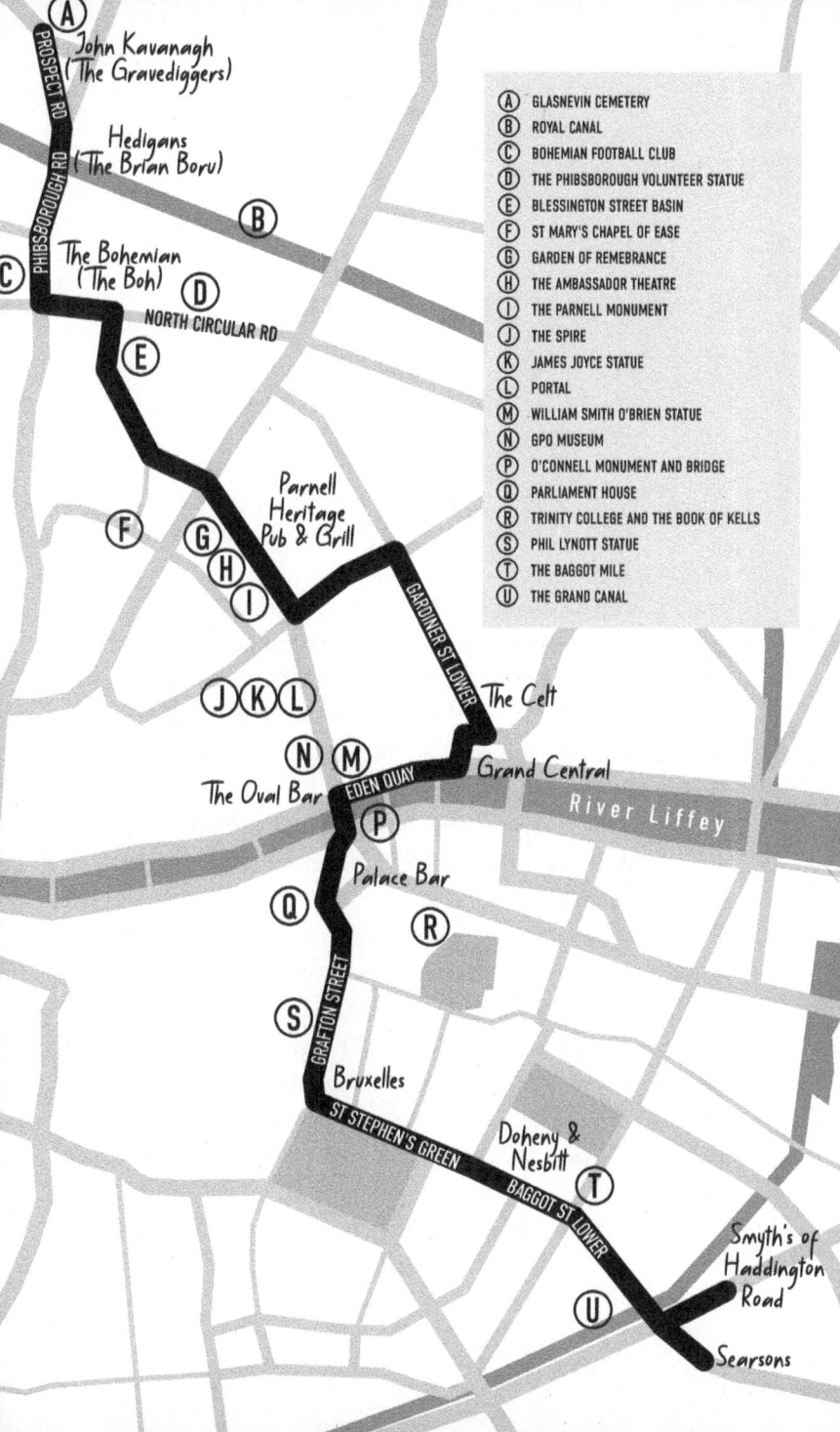

DIRECTIONS

Start at **John Kavanagh (1, A)** before heading south along Prospect Avenue. Keep going, crossing over the main road, until you reach **Hedigans (2)** on the right-hand side. Continue past the pub and over the Royal Canal **(B)**, with the football ground's **(C)** lights towering over the buildings, before coming to **The Bohemian (3)** on the corner.

Follow the road east past Doyle Corner and turn down the tree-lined avenue that has the Phibsborough Volunteer statue **(D)** in front of it.

Do not miss the stone archway on the left that opens into Blessington Street Basin **(E)**. Pass through this and take the first right upon reaching the road and first junction.

At St Mary's Chapel of Ease **(F)** turn left and it is then a decent walk with the Garden of Remembrance **(G)** on the left.

At the end, where there is a busy main road, **Parnell Heritage Pub & Grill (4)** is on the opposite side of the road to the left.

Past the pub, turn right at the main road **(H, I)** before turning left at the *Spire* **(J, K, L)**, where **The Celt (5)** is on the right-hand side. Head back to the main road and go towards the river, where **Grand Central (6)** is on the corner opposite the statue of William Smith O'Brien **(M)**. On the other side of the main road is **The Oval Bar (7)** and further down towards the river is the GPO Museum **(N)**, which was the site of the 1916 Easter Rising **(O)**. Past the O'Connell Monument and Bridge **(P)** follow the right-hand fork in the road, where **Palace Bar (8)** is at the end of the first left. Keep on the main road as it bends right, then left between Parliament House **(Q)** and Trinity College **(R)**, heading down the pedestrian area of Grafton Street before the road bends left.

Down the third right, past the statue of Phil Lynott **(S)**, is **Bruxelles (9)**.

Continue down Grafton Street until the end, where a left turn heads alongside the park to **Doheny & Nesbitt (10)** on the left-hand side.

Head further along the Baggot Mile **(T)** and over the Grand Canal **(U)**, where **Smyth's of Haddington Road (11)** is down the first right, with **Searsons (12)** back on the main road, a little further along.

---

1. JOHN KAVANAGH (THE GRAVEDIGGERS)

There is not a 'pub influencer' with any credibility that has not been to this famous pub. Founded in 1833, it is still run by the Kavanagh family.

Its unique location, built into the side of the cemetery wall, made it a popular destination when there was a funeral. When the council closed the adjacent entrance, the cemetery workers, who were now unable to easily access the pub, would knock on the wall with their shovels and line up along the railings waiting for their pints of Guinness.

Inside the pub is like stepping back in time and it is easy to miss the intimate snug to the right of the entrance, which would have been where wives and girlfriends sat. It is very rare to get an opportunity to sit in here.

The first section of the pub would have been a convenience store, with the original drawers behind the bar containing items like rice, tea and coffee. The high, swinging saloon doors prevented customers from observing the drinkers at the rear of the bar, and have been preserved despite plans to replace them as the population's average height has since increased!

Not only is the pub famous for its Guinness – it is often proclaimed one of the best in Dublin – it also serves traditional Irish food such as white coddle, which consists of white sausage in a stew, with landlord Ciaran claiming that every family has its own version of the dish.

The walls and ceilings have not been redecorated for more than thirty years, and the smoke from years gone by has left a deep yellow hue throughout.

I love this pub and have been lucky enough to visit on several occasions – the first time with notable Irish pub expert, Cassie Stokes, who managed to secure us a couple of pints of plain in the snug.

It's impossible to talk about where to find the best pints of Guinness without mentioning this famous pub.

A. GLASNEVIN CEMETERY

Established in 1832 by Daniel O'Connell, one of Ireland's greatest historical figures, this is Ireland's largest burial ground.

Its vast 124 acres is the final resting place for more than 1.5 million people, with many prominent figures from Irish history among them, including the revolutionary Michael Collins, Countess Constance Markievicz, who was the first woman elected to British Parliament, trade union leader James Larking, and Dubliners founding member Luke Kelly.

O'Connell, who earned the nickname 'The Liberator', is buried here too, with the eponymous O'Connell memorial tower – the tallest round tower in Ireland – standing close by, offering those visitors fit enough to climb it panoramic views of the city.

Before the cemetery was established, Irish Catholics had faced restrictions on their burial rites. A popular champion against injustice and oppression, O'Connell founded Glasnevin to provide a burial place for all, regardless of faith.

Eleven-year-old Michael Carey was the first person buried here, on 22 February 1832.

2. HEDIGANS (THE BRIAN BORU)

Often a convenient stop for funeral processions, this pub has stood here for more than two centuries and lays claim to having the oldest beer garden in Dublin.

While it still holds the name of the family that ran the pub and adjacent grocery store, it is commonly referred to as the Brian Boru after the legendary King of Ireland who was said to have camped on this site ahead of his victory over the Vikings at the Battle of Clontarf in 1014.

Although much of the pub and its windows have been refurbished, the original mirrored signs that would have been at the front of the pub have now been moved inside and are among the few remaining examples in Dublin.

B. ROYAL CANAL

This historic waterway stretches for approximately 90 miles, from Spencer Dock in Dublin to Richmond Harbour in Cloondara, out in County Longford, where it connects with the River Shannon.

It was constructed between 1790 and 1817 to move freight and passengers between central Ireland and the city.

C. BOHEMIAN FOOTBALL CLUB

Dublin's oldest football club was established on 6 September (my birthday) in 1890 (obvs not my birth year).

Although first playing at Phoenix Park, in their traditional red and black, they earned the nickname 'The Gypsies' as it was not until 1901 that they moved to their permanent home at Dalymount Park in Phibsborough, with the ground often referred to as the 'spiritual home of Irish football'.

One of the most decorated clubs in Irish football history, they have won eleven League of Ireland titles, seven FAI Cups and three League Cups.

Their most notable victory came under manager Billy Young, when 'The Bohs' ran out 3–2 winners over Glasgow Rangers in 1984, leaving Young's tenure to be remembered as a golden era for the club.

3. THE BOHEMIAN

Given its location, it is no surprise that this pub caters for fans visiting the nearby Bohemian FC ground, and it is affectionately known as 'The Boh'.

Although it was established in 1887, rebuilt in 1906 and has retained much of its original décor, it is perhaps best loved for its narrow beer garden and first-floor terrace, which is one of the best places to catch the sun.

It sits on Doyle's Corner opposite another pub with which it used to share owners – going so far as to have been connected by a tunnel until the new owners blocked it up under the suspicion that they were stealing customers.

A popular spot with football fans on their way to a match.

D. THE PHIBSBOROUGH VOLUNTEER STATUE

Officially known as the Irish Volunteer Monument, this statue pays tribute to the members of the Dublin Brigade of the Irish Volunteers who were involved in the Easter Rising and the War of Independence between 1916 and 1921.

Sculptor Leo Broe – himself a former volunteer – crafted the figure of a soldier clutching his rifle from Irish limestone. Fully restored in 1991, the rifle had previously been absent for many years after vandals desecrated the statue in the 1970s.

Unveiled in 1939 in front of a crowd of more than three thousand, it was originally intended to function as a drinking fountain; however, its water feature has since been decommissioned.

E. BLESSINGTON STREET BASIN

Sometimes referred to as the Dublin's 'secret garden', the basin was constructed between 1803 and 1810 to supply clean water to the city's north side. Then called the Royal George Reservoir, the basin held approximately 3.3 million gallons of water.

The rapidly expanding population quickly outgrew the basin's capacity and by the late nineteenth century, the local authority took steps to convert the reservoir into a public park.

Alongside serving the population, the reserves were diverted to serve local industries, including whiskey distilleries, with the most notable being Jameson's in Smithfield.

Be warned, though: if, like my camera assistant Chloe, you have a fear of birds, you might like to walk around the outside, as the garden is a popular place for many different varieties.

F. ST MARY'S CHAPEL OF EASE

More commonly known as the Black Church, this striking former Church of Ireland was constructed in 1830 by architect John Semple, who received funding from the Board of First Fruits, which was responsible for building and improving the local churches during that period.

Its nickname derives from the dark 'Calp' limestone that was used in its construction, which appears black when it rains.

The congregation began to decline and, by 1962, the church had been deconsecrated and repurposed into office space.

Local legend says that walking around the church three times at midnight while reciting the 'Hail Mary' backwards summons the devil. But we've no time for that – we've got pubs to get to.

G. GARDEN OF REMEMBRANCE

The location where the Irish Volunteers were founded in 1913, it was opened in 1966 on the fiftieth anniversary of the Easter Rising and also commemorates other significant events in Irish history, including rebellions from 1798 to the 1921 War of Independence.

At the northern end of the garden is a sculpture of the Children of Lir, which was added in 1971 and takes inspiration from the Irish myth that describes how four children were transformed into swans for nine hundred years.

4. PARNELL HERITAGE PUB & GRILL

After a last-minute change of plan due to a pub closure, we were lucky to stumble across this pub with its chatty landlord who was full of stories.

It takes its name from the prominent Irish nationalist leader Charles Stewart Parnell, who was often referred to as the 'uncrowned king of Ireland' and was a regular patron, having attended nearby political rallies.

Although the pub was built in 1879, there has been a licence on the premises since the 1780s and over the years it has been a popular, upmarket hangout for many political figures who had residences in the street.

If the weather is nice, be sure to pop up to the roof terrace.

H. THE AMBASSADOR THEATRE

When it was built in 1764 it would have been part of the Rotunda Hospital complex, serving as an assembly hall designed to raise income for the hospital.

By 1897, the venue had begun to host movie screenings, which would have been very rare at the time, before it became a full-time cinema known as the Rotunda in 1910.

After its capacity was extended to 1,200 seats in the 1950s, the cinema continued to operate under its current name until 1999, when it was repurposed as a live music venue from 2001 to 2008, going on to host notable artists such as Amy Winehouse and Queens of the Stone Age.

I. THE PARNELL MONUMENT

Born in 1846, Charles Stewart Parnell led the Irish Parliamentary Party and was a pivotal figure in the quest for Irish independence.

The monument was unveiled on 1 October 1911, with the outstretched arms symbolising Parnell's oratory expertise. The large obelisk next to it bears a gilded harp and an inscription from one of Parnell's speeches: 'No man has a right to fix the boundary to the march of a nation ... We have never attempted to fix the *ne plus ultra* to the progress of Ireland's nationhood, and we never shall.'

J. THE *SPIRE*

Dominating the city's skyline, this striking stainless-steel sculpture is the world's tallest piece of free-standing public art at a whopping 393 feet tall.

While it is officially known as the Monument of Light, locals have coined several comical nicknames for it, with the 'safest' being the Stiletto in the Ghetto, the Stiffy by the Liffey, the Erection at the Intersection, the Rod to God and the Pin in the Bin. The last being a nod to what many Dubliners believed to be a waste of public funds.

K. JAMES JOYCE STATUE

This prominent bronze sculpture of the famed Irish novelist was unveiled on 16 June 1990 to commemorate 'Bloomsday' – the day on which Joyce's novel *Ulysses* is set.

Just like the *Spire* nearby, locals have also dubbed it with a cheeky nickname: 'The Prick with the Stick'.

L. PORTAL

This groundbreaking interactive public art installation, which opened in May 2024, originally created a real-time connection between Dublin and New York before the latter portal was closed and moved to Philadelphia. Here it was relaunched with livestream connections to Dublin along with Vilnius in Lithuania and Lublin in Poland.

Although now non-operational, it remains next to the statue of Joyce, having sadly been switched off at the end of January 2025, with its future unclear.

5. THE CELT

It is easy to get stuck in the tiny bar at the front of this pub and miss the large area at the back, which was originally constructed as a horse stable in 1864.

The stable became Ireland's first ever trade union hall ahead of the first strikes of 1913, where Jim Larkin, better known as 'Big Jim', held meetings with union members.

A few years later, in 1920, it was repurposed into a dance hall before falling into disrepair and serving as a storeroom for the nearby Guineys department store for nearly one hundred years.

I love how the walls are completely packed with memorabilia and murals as the tiny front bar opens into the expansive extension underneath the original Belfast-style ceiling brackets.

6. GRAND CENTRAL

Originally two buildings until the Munster & Leinster Bank acquired number 11, which was originally a tailor's shop, in 1926.

During the 1916 Easter Rising, the British gunboat *Helga* unleashed a barrage of shells from the River Liffey, which made contact with the General Post Office (GPO) building and devastated the surrounding area.

After extensive repairs, number 10 operated as a bank from 1917 until it was acquired by the Louis Fitzgerald Group and converted into a pub in 2001.

It is notable as the site of what is regarded as the first-ever pirate radio broadcast, as revolutionaries used the wireless telegraphy station on this site to declare the Irish Republic in 1916.

M. WILLIAM SMITH O'BRIEN STATUE

A key figure in Ireland's nineteenth-century nationalist movement and the 1848 rebellion, O'Brien was a leader of Young Ireland.

Although the uprising was unsuccessful, the statue was unveiled in 1870 to honour his life, legacy and dedication to Irish self-governance. It is notable as the first public monument in Dublin to commemorate someone who had taken up arms for Irish independence.

7. THE OVAL BAR

The only survivor of the bombardment of this area from the River Liffey during the 1916 uprising, this 1820 building was famously photographed standing alone alongside the rubble, enshrining its legacy as the only licensed premises in the Abbey Street area to have remained in its original location.

It was meticulously restored in 1917, with an ornate décor that spans three floors, and with the seven men who signed the Proclamation of the Irish Republic commemorated by busts that feature in its bay window.

It is owned by the family-run Chawke Pub Group, whose founder Bill opened his first pub in Adare in 1959.

I've fond memories of sitting on the first floor, which is the best place to sit, with Ian Dowling of *Irish Pickers* TV series fame and enjoying a few Guinness while looking down onto the busy bar and, on the occasion of my last visit, my camera assistant Chloe and I stopped by for traditional Irish stew while we charged our cameras.

N. GPO MUSEUM

The former General Post Office (GPO), designed by architect Francis Johnston and opened in 1818, is one of Dublin's most iconic buildings, both architecturally and historically.

Featuring a grand granite portico, it was constructed in the neoclassical Greek Revival style, with its six Ionic columns and a central pediment casting an imposing presence at the heart of Dublin.

Originally intended as the city's main postal hub, it became renowned for its central role in the 1916 Easter Rising, after republican leaders including Patrick Pearse and James Connolly seized the building on Easter Monday and converted it into their headquarters during the armed insurrection against British rule.

With the Irish tricolour raised above, it came under heavy shelling during the fighting that followed, leaving just the stone façade intact.

Gutted by fire, the building lay in ruins for many years, and it was not until 1929 that it was restored and reopened to the public.

While it may remain synonymous with Irish resilience and national identity, it now operates once again in the role for which it was originally intended, as a post office.

O. 1916 EASTER RISING

Beginning on Easter Monday 1916, a group of around 1,200 Irish nationalists staged an armed insurrection with the aim of establishing an independent Irish Republic while Britain was distracted by World War I.

The uprising was planned in secret by the Irish Republican Brotherhood, leading to the capture of several key locations in the city. These included the General Post Office, which became their headquarters, and it was from there that Patrick Pearse read the Proclamation of the Irish Republic, to declare Ireland's independence.

Fighting and gunfire raged in the streets of Dublin for six days, the British Army responding with formidable force. They deployed thousands of troops accompanied by heavy artillery, and sent a gunboat up the River Liffey to shell much of the city centre.

The rebels were outnumbered and lacking supplies. With the bombardment also costing the lives of many civilians, local support rapidly disintegrated and by Saturday 29 April the leaders had surrendered.

Most of the 485 people killed were civilians, with more than 2,600 wounded. A British firing squad executed fifteen leaders, including Pearse and the seven signatories of the Proclamation.

Although support had declined during the uprising, the executions, carried out with such severity, profoundly shocked the Irish public and the Easter Rising, although a military failure, became a moral and symbolic victory for Irish republicanism.

Public opinion shifted towards the rebels and there was a surge in support for the republic, leading to the Irish War of Independence, which eventually led to the establishment of the Irish Free State in 1922.

In recent times, the Easter Rising has come to be celebrated as a foundational moment for modern Ireland, and the occasion is marked with events and remembrance throughout Dublin.

P. O'CONNELL MONUMENT AND BRIDGE

Another prominent landmark at the heart of the scene of the uprising is this statue and bridge named after Daniel O'Connell, the nineteenth-century political leader who earned the moniker 'The Liberator' for his role in winning political rights for Irish Catholics in 1829.

Unveiled in 1882, the monument features more than thirty figures representing Irish culture, with the four winged figures at its base symbolising Patriotism, Fidelity, Eloquence and Justice.

There has been a bridge opposite since 1791; however, it was redesigned, widened and flattened in the late nineteenth century to cope with the city's increasing traffic, before being renamed O'Connell Bridge at the same time as the monument's unveiling.

Can you spot the unusual fact about this bridge, which has the rare feature of being as wide as it is long?

8. PALACE BAR

Almost every local will mention this Victorian pub as one of the most beautiful in Dublin.

It sits at the edge of the popular Temple Bar, and is notable for its literary associations with the likes of Patrick Kavanagh, Brendan Behan and Flann O'Brien.

I was unable to squeeze into the tiny snug at the end of the bar on my visit, although it can hold around five people and is said to have been the location of Michael Collins' meetings during the Irish War of Independence.

Look out at the rear of the pub and you'll see a picture of

NYC's famous McSorley's Old Ale House and its iconic catchphrase, 'Be Good or Be Gone.'

I filmed here with Cassie Stokes, who is well known as the authority on Irish pubs, and there was quite a crowd taking pictures as we chatted outside – probably my first/only taste of celebrity life in Ireland.

One of Ireland's most beautiful pubs.

Q. PARLIAMENT HOUSE

Constructed between 1729 and 1739, it was the world's first purpose-built bicameral legislature – which means a parliament divided into two chambers, like the House of Commons and the House of Lords.

It housed the Irish Parliament until the Act of Union in 1801, which merged the Kingdom of Ireland and the Kingdom of Great Britain, thereby dissolving Irish legislation. After that it was sold to the Bank of Ireland in 1803, with significant alterations leaving only the House of Lords chamber remaining for today's tourists.

R. TRINITY COLLEGE AND THE BOOK OF KELLS

Despite the 'College' in its name, this is in fact Ireland's oldest university and is officially known as the College of the Holy and Undivided Trinity of Queen Elizabeth Near Dublin.

It was founded through a royal charter of Queen Elizabeth I in 1592, on the site of the former Priory of All Hallows, primarily aimed at educating the protestant elite.

The college is notable for its Old Library, housing the Long Room and the *Book of Kells* – a ninth-century illuminated manuscript (like a medieval comic book of detail) of the Gospels – which draws thousands of visitors each year.

The Book of Kells is one of the country's most treasured cultural artefacts, considered a masterpiece of medieval illuminated manuscript art, created as it was by Celtic monks around 800 CE.

Containing the four Gospels of the New Testament – Matthew, Mark, Luke and John – it is written in Latin, and accompanied by elaborate and colourful illustrations that have been well preserved.

The origins of the book are unclear but are believed to trace back to a monastery on the Scottish island of Iona, with the book being completed at the Abbey of Kells in County Meath, the monks having fled Iona to avoid Viking raids.

Its ornate design means that the manuscript was originally intended for ceremonial use on church altars. The extraordinary detail encompasses entire pages devoted to single words or initials, surrounded by intricate patterns, with the Chi Rho page considered one of the most beautiful in the history of manuscript illumination, and one of Europe's most significantly important medieval artefacts.

Although unaccounted for during much of the medieval period, the book was rediscovered and gifted to Trinity College Dublin in 1661 for safekeeping.

These days it is usually kept on display, in a temperature-controlled case, showing both an illustrated page and a text page.

S. PHIL LYNOTT STATUE

One of Ireland's most iconic rock musicians, and best known as the frontman of Thin Lizzy, the distinctive bass player is instantly recognisable due to his tall frame and masses of hair.

Born in 1949 in West Bromwich, England, to an Irish mother and Guyanese father, Lynott's charisma, poetic lyrics and pioneering role as a Black Irish rock star left an indelible mark on the world music scene. He was famously once asked what it was like to be Black and Irish, to which he replied, 'Like a pint of Guinness.'

Tragically, the 'ace with the bass' passed away in 1986 at only thirty-six years old due to complications following years of substance abuse.

Unveiled in 2005, the statue was sculpted by Paul Daly and cast by Leo Higgins.

9. BRUXELLES

Originally known as the Grafton Mooney – as part of a chain – from its establishment in 1886, the pub was renamed in 1973 to celebrate Ireland's entry into the European Economic Community.

It is notable as a hub for the emerging music scene of the

1960s and 1970s, and still holds an affinity with legendary Thin Lizzy frontman Phil Lynott, who is immortalised in the bar with several murals.

Split into three distinctive bars, the main saloon area features the original tile work, with the Zodiac and Flanders bars downstairs catering for live music and dancing.

One of Ireland's most famous sons is honoured with this statue just off Grafton Street.

10. DOHENY & NESBITT

A distinctive landmark on the famous Baggott Mile, it was opened in the 1840s and has retained many original features such as the carved timber, aged floors and an ornate ceiling that is crafted from papier mâché.

It was originally called Delahunty's before it was taken over by Felix Connolly in the 1950s, with the mirror on the rear bar still bearing his name.

The pub spans several floors that feature an opulently refurbished whiskey bar, and it is one of the favourite pubs of Daragh Curran (better known as 'The Guinness Guru') with it being a staple of the area's '12 Pubs of Christmas' event.

T. THE BAGGOT MILE

A key destination in the notorious '12 Pubs of Christmas' event, mainly due to the area's dense concentration of pubs, the origin of the nickname lies in the tongue-in-cheek idea that you could visit a pub roughly every few steps along the street.

Where there are pubs there are writers, and in the mid-1900s, the area became popular with legendary figures such as Patrick Kavanagh, Brendan Behan and Flann O'Brien, who were often spotted drinking and debating in the local pubs.

The area was also a notable destination for civil servants and politicians, given its proximity to local government buildings.

U. THE GRAND CANAL

It is hard to believe that this historic waterway stretches right across Ireland, all the way to the River Shannon in the west.

Spanning a whopping 82 miles separated by forty-three locks, its construction took nearly fifty years, from 1756 to its completion in 1804. The canal project was conceived as a vital means of connection to transport goods and passengers across the country.

In more recent times, the Grand Canal Dock area, at the heart of Dublin, has received significant investment from numerous global tech companies, earning it the tongue-in-cheek nickname 'Silicon Docks'.

11. SMYTH'S OF HADDINGTON ROAD

This cosy pub was run by the Smyth family, who lived above it for forty-seven years prior to the current owners taking over.

In 1999 it gained notoriety as the first pub in the world to be purchased via an internet auction, as an audience of more than five thousand people logged in to see one hundred potential buyers exceed the £2.5 million reserve price to reach £3.35 million – one of the most expensive acquisitions in the capital at the time.

It is hard to imagine this old, traditional family pub having such an innovative history – especially if you are lucky enough to have sat in the snug, which is where Daragh, better known as the Guinness Guru, and I sat when we visited on our pub crawl.

Sharing a pint of plain with a pal in an old Irish snug is one of life's pleasures.

12. SEARSONS

Originally Henry Tobin's Grocer, Wine & Spirit Merchant, it thrived in Victorian Dublin due to its prime location and prosperous clientele.

Despite this success it was converted into a pub in 1884,

when William Davy took over, and became a hub for writers, journalists and politicians.

Patrick Kavanagh, one of Ireland's greatest poets, was a regular during the 1940s and 1950s, stopping in after selling poems to the *Irish Times*. His love for Hilda Moriarty inspired the poem 'On Raglan Road'. However, he later fell out of favour due to his tumultuous friendship with Brendan Behan, who was notorious for his wit and vulgarity.

William and Michael Searson took over in 1923 and ran the pub until William's death in 1959, after which it was sold in 1961 to the Hardy family for £30,000.

Today, it is famous for its whiskey collection, including its own variety, which is distilled in small batches and sold for €3,500 a bottle.

At the end of our day's filming of this route, Chloe and I were lucky enough to take the prime seats, in the tiny snug at the end of the bar, to enjoy a personal whiskey-tasting session!

At the end of a long days filming, Chloe and I had earned our drinks.

GALWAY
(Latin Quarter to Eyre Square)

One of the most popular destinations in Ireland for tourists, mainly due to its vibrant night life, it is hard to believe that within the medieval walls was originally a small, industrious fishing town.

Everything is very walkable and although it is one of Ireland's five cities, it still feels very much like a small, friendly town – even if it is buzzing with tourists.

This route loops out of the centre to take in the modern cathedral and the rivers, before heading into the heart of the Latin Quarter, which buzzes with activity almost 24/7.

I particularly loved the trad music sessions in most pubs, and the beer gardens of Carroll's, O'Connell's and An Púcán, which are so good it is difficult to choose a favourite – so make sure each one gets a visit!

Start at Tig Cóilí (H91 XR50).

1. **Tig Cóilí** *12.30 p.m.*
24 Mainguard Street, H91 XR50

2. **Sally Longs Rock Bar** *1.15 p.m.*
33 Abbeygate Street Upper, H91 F2RV

3. **Carroll's Bar** *2.30 p.m.*
39 Dominick Street Lower, H91 RX83

4. **Monroe's** *3.00 p.m.*
14 Dominick Street Upper, H91 WD2H

5. **The Salt House** *3.30 p.m.*
4 Raven Terrace, H91 D9Y2

6. **The Quays Bar & Music Hall** *4.15 p.m.*
11 Quay Street, H91 V53F

7. **The Kings Head** *5.00 p.m.*
15 High Street, H91 AY6P

8. **Taaffes Bar** *5.30 p.m.*
20 Shop Street, H91 WF20

9. **Garavan's Bar** *6.15 p.m.*
46 William Street, H91 RX54

10. **The Hole in the Wall** *7.00 p.m.*
17 Eyre Street, Galway, H91 E8K8

11. **The Skeff Late Bar & Kitchen** *7.45 p.m.*
27 Eyre Square, H91 CFX5

12. **O'Connell's Bar** *8.30 p.m.*
Eyre Square, H91 FT22

13. **An Púcán** *9.15 p.m.*
11 Forster Street, Galway, H91 P65D

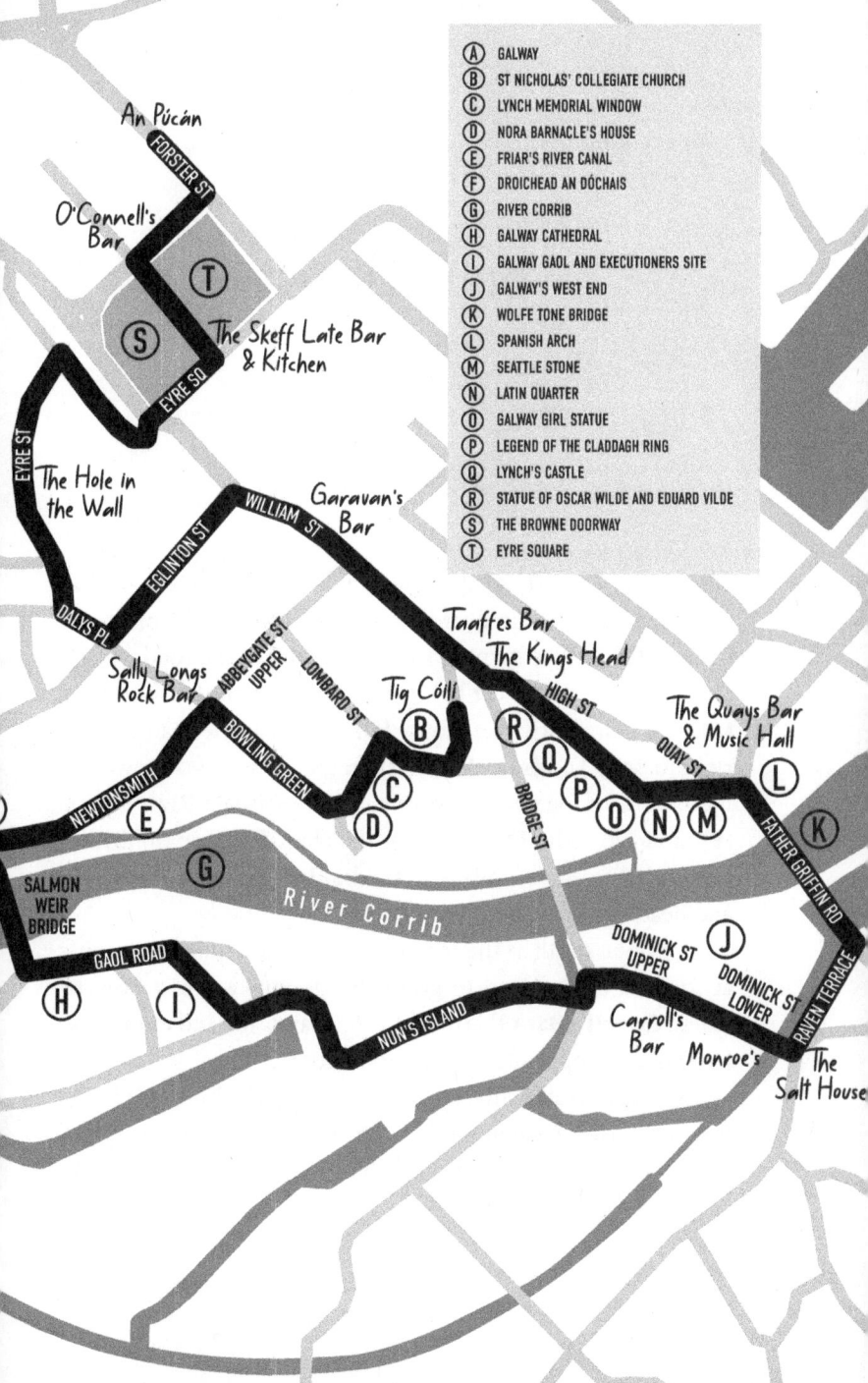

DIRECTIONS

Start at **Tig Cóilí (1, A)** then, leaving through the rear of the pub, turn left on Churchyard Street past St Nicholas' Collegiate Church **(B)**, before turning right at the end of the road.

Take the first left just before the Lynch Memorial Window **(C)**, past Nora Barnacles House **(D)**. Follow as the road curves right to **Sally Longs Rock Bar (2)** on the corner. Head towards the river, with the mural at your back, along Friar's River Canal **(E)**, and cross the Droichead an Dóchais **(F)** over the River Corrib **(G)** towards Galway Cathedral **(H)**, before turning left and heading through the car park **(I)**.

Continue south as the road curves, before a quick left/right at the end of the road to go down Dominick Street Lower, where **Carroll's Bar (3)** is on the right-hand side and **Monroe's (4, J)** is at the opposite the end of the road.

Exit the pub along the river, where **The Salt House (5)** is on the right. After leaving the pub, cross Wolfe Tone Bridge **(K)**, where the Spanish Arch **(L)** can be spotted on the other side of the river on the right.

Pass the Seattle Stone **(M)** and head into the Latin Quarter **(N)**, where the Galway Girl statue **(O)** is outside **The Quay's Bar & Music Hall (6)** on the right. Continue along the road, past the Legend of the Claddagh Ring Visitor Centre **(P)**, and on to **The Kings Head (7)** and **Taaffes Bar (8)**, passing Lynch's Castle **(Q)** on the left before **Garavan's Bar (9)**.

Turn left past the statue of Oscar Wilde and Eduard Vilde **(R)**, before turning right at the next junction and following the road right to **The Hole in the Wall (10)**.

Continue past the pub before emerging at the Browne Doorway **(S)**, where **The Skeff Late Bar & Kitchen (11)** is on the right of Eyre Square **(T)**, with **O'Connell's Bar (12)** opposite on the left. The final pub, **An Púcán (13)**, can be found around the corner.

---

1. TIG CÓILÍ

Located at the heart of the vibrant Latin Quarter, this pub is loved mostly due to its affinity with music, as trad sessions are held twice daily all year round.

The walls are adorned with photographs of well-known musicians and celebrities who have visited over the years and include stained-glass tributes to local musicians Séamus Begley and Desmond O'Halloran, who were regulars at the pub.

Begley, who was well known as a singer and accordion player, passed away in 2023, four years after singer and fiddle player O'Halloran.

I bumped into some American travellers from Boston on my visit, and supped my Guinness while they tried to convince me of their Irish heritage.

A. GALWAY

Granted city status in 1484 by King Richard III, by royal charter, Galway received a mayor and a degree of self-governance that elevated its independent status.

It is often called the 'City of the Tribes', after the fourteen families that dominated the political and commercial functions of the city between the fifteenth and seventeenth centuries following the royal change.

It is famous for its medieval streets, traditional Irish music in almost every pub and the influx of tourists – especially from the USA.

Originally a small fishing town, it is the gateway to the Wild Atlantic Way, which is one of the longest defined coastal driving routes in the world.

Galway was an important fishing location, with its traditional sailing boat, the Galway hooker, evolving from smaller fishing vessels. The boat's distinctive look is due to the dark black pitch painted on the hull, and its red or rust-coloured sails due to the natural coating made from tree bark that is used to preserve the canvas.

Intrinsically connected to music and the arts, it hosts the Galway International Arts Festival and was (of course) the filming location for the video that accompanied Ed Sheeran's hit song 'Galway Girl' – more on that later in the route.

B. ST NICHOLAS' COLLEGIATE CHURCH

One of the oldest medieval churches in Ireland that is still in use today, it was built in 1320 and is dedicated to St Nicholas, who was the patron saint of sailors.

C. LYNCH MEMORIAL WINDOW

There is a tragic tale behind the remaining stonework of the family home of James Lynch FitzStephen, who served as mayor in 1493.

Renowned for his strict adherence to the law, legend has it that when his son, Walter, murdered a Spanish merchant named Pedro in a jealous rage over the woman he loved, Lynch was unable to find an executioner to serve the punishment.

So, in a defiant example of applying equal justice to all, the mayor sentenced his son to the gallows and personally hung him from the window of their family home.

D. NORA BARNACLE'S HOUSE

This otherwise unremarkable building was the childhood home of Nora Barnacle, who was the wife and muse of Irish author James Joyce.

Born in 1884, Nora is believed to have been the inspiration for Molly Bloom in Joyce's seminal work *Ulysses*.

The modest two-room house, where she used to live with her mother and six siblings, has since been converted into what is believed to be Ireland's smallest museum.

2. SALLY LONGS ROCK BAR

It is impossible to miss the striking mural on the side of this legendary rock music venue, which was established in 1988.

While the artwork and memorabilia continue throughout, the most impressive piece is that painted on the gable wall by Ciarán Dunlevy in 2007. It is structured into three distinct sections. The lower part showcases living legends such as Eric Clapton, Bono, Slash, Axl Rose and Brian May; above them are now departed legends such as Jimi Hendrix, Jim Morrison and Johnny Cash; while the top section pays homage to Michelangelo's *The Creation of Adam*, with Elvis Presley reaching out to touch god.

Sadly, since its installation, living legends Prince and Tina Turner have also died.

E. FRIAR'S RIVER CANAL

This man-made channel, sometimes referred to as Friar's Cut, was created in 1178 to provide a route for boats between Lough Corrib and the sea at Galway.

F. DROICHEAD AN DÓCHAIS

Translating to 'Bridge of Hope' in English, good luck pronouncing the Gaelic name of this pedestrian and cycle bridge. It opened in May 2023, making it the first new bridge installed over the River Corrib in over thirty years.

G. RIVER CORRIB

One of the shortest rivers in Europe at 3.7 miles long, its diminutive nature is deceiving as its powerful flow discharges more water than almost any other in Ireland, with only the vast River Shannon being larger.

Its name comes from the legend of Gaillimh, daughter of a Fir Bolg chieftain, who drowned in the river.

H. GALWAY CATHEDRAL

Officially named the Cathedral of Our Lady Assumed into Heaven & St Nicholas, this Roman Catholic cathedral was constructed in 1965, on the site of the former city prison, making it one of the newest stone cathedrals in Europe.

I. GALWAY GAOL AND EXECUTIONERS SITE

The original Galway jail was built on the site where Galway Cathedral now stands. It housed prisoners and death row inmates between 1810 and 1939.

It closed as the building had become dilapidated due to overcrowding and poor sanitation, and due to a change in the penal system following Irish independence, with all inmates moving to Limerick.

Hidden among the car parking spaces is a raised area that was used to host public executions, which is where Myles Joyce was executed at the age of forty and buried under what is now the car park.

His alleged involvement in the 'Maamtrasna murders' is a tragic tale of one of Ireland's most infamous miscarriages of justice.

On the night of 17 August 1882, several members of a branch of his family were killed and, following his arrest alongside nine other men, Myles Joyce was reported to have confessed, despite speaking very little to no English. The case was subsequently heard in English without any translation service, with three of the men – including Myles Joyce – sentenced to death.

Shortly before the three were executed, his co-accused admitted their guilt but emphasised Myles Joyce's innocence.

Following an expert legal review of his case, he was issued with a formal pardon in 2018 by then President Michael D. Higgins.

3. CARROLL'S BAR

Famous for its beer garden, which contains a double decker bus, and it's easy to see why. I do enjoy the way some of the pubs I cover in this book create almost a mini-village in their gardens.

It is affectionately known as the Caravan Club, with food being served from the bus and a DJ booth on top of a mocked-up pulpit, complete with a massive fake organ.

It's impossible to miss the giant altar in the garden which is perfect for DJs.

4. MONROE'S

This striking corner pub, set across several floors, was established in 1964 and is a renowned family-owned pub at the heart of Galway's vibrant Westend.

Originally Monroe's New Manhattan Bar, the main pub was opened by John and Margaret Monroe on their return from New York City. It became the first in Galway to offer table service, a 'Ladies Lounge' and a 'Singing Lounge'.

The pub is split into several areas; next door is their other bar, McBride's & Co, which has been created in the theme of an old apothecary, and upstairs, the building also includes a live music venue that can host up to six hundred revellers.

J. GALWAY'S WESTEND

Boasting colourful street art, and just a few minutes from the more touristy centre of the Latin Quarter, this area is a popular hub for the live music scene and the centre of the International Arts Festival.

5. THE SALT HOUSE

Part of the Galway Bay Brewery family, this cosy pub is more like a craft beer taproom. When I was there, they had an impressive selection of more than 120 bottled and canned craft beers from around the world.

It was quite comical during my visit as a group of more than a dozen sweating folks from the local running club turned up, with the pub being a destination on their route.

Personally, I am much happier walking the routes than even contemplating running them!

K. WOLFE TONE BRIDGE

Named after Irish icon Theobald Wolfe Tone, who was a leading figure in the Irish Rebellion of 1798, the original bridge was replaced in 1887 as the city grew and demands on the thoroughfare increased.

Late-night revellers should be wary of a local legend which

claims that a large black dog with 'fiery eyes' and 'snow white sharp teeth' emerges from the river to prey on people crossing the bridge after midnight.

L. SPANISH ARCH

A remnant of Galway's medieval history, it was erected in 1584 as an extension to the existing town wall that had stood since twelfth-century Norman times and been given the name 'Ceann an Bhalla', meaning 'head of the wall'.

It was partially destroyed in 1755, when a tsunami resulting from the Lisbon earthquake travelled more than 1,100 nautical miles to damage the city walls and nearby coastline.

M. SEATTLE STONE

Marking the official twinning between the two cities that occurred in 1986, this granite stone was unveiled in 1993.

Both are coastal cities, with a rich history of seafaring and the arts, and there is not much more to it than that. Perhaps it is also there to acknowledge the American tourists that descend on Ireland all year round to trace their family heritage.

N. LATIN QUARTER

Part of the original city centre, which would have been surrounded by walls, this area preserves much of Galway's famed medieval architecture.

Along Kirwan's Lane are restored sixteenth- and seventeenth-century buildings that showcase the city's long history.

Although the name of the area implies a flair and vibrancy that is indeed on show today, it most likely has its roots in the city's wealthy elite, who would have spoken Latin.

O. GALWAY GIRL STATUE

Unveiled in 2022, this statue in the busy high street portrays a young girl in traditional attire.

Popularised in the eponymous song by Ed Sheeran, where he enjoys a relationship with a carefree local girl, Galway girls are stereotypically free-spirited, with Irish charm and the unusual combination of jet-black hair and piercing blue eyes.

6. THE QUAYS BAR & MUSIC HALL

With a legacy spanning nearly four hundred years, this is one of the city's oldest pubs, and boasts an interior complete with restored gothic arches, stained-glass windows and reconditioned church pews that were removed from an old cathedral.

P. LEGEND OF THE CLADDAGH RING

Originating from the Claddagh area of Galway, this traditional ring is seen as a symbol of love, loyalty and friendship.

The distinctive design features two hands, representing friendship, clasping a heart to symbolise love, topped with a crown to stand for loyalty.

While the ring may be used as a wedding or engagement ring, its placement is significant. When worn on the right hand, with the point of the heart facing outwards, this means the wearer is open to love, but if it is pointing inwards then they are in a relationship. Following a similar theme on the left hand, pointing out means engaged and pointing in means married.

7. THE KINGS HEAD

Owned and operated by the Grealish family since 1989, this pub's long history is said to stretch back nearly eight hundred years.

Records imply that it was seized when Oliver Cromwell recaptured Ireland in the mid-seventeenth century and went on to install Colonel Peter Stubbers – who was not from one of Galway's fourteen family 'tribes' – as the city's first mayor.

While there is no specific evidence, rumours persist that this was the reward for Stubbers's part in the execution of King Charles I. There are two 'thrones' by the entrance, overlooking a fireplace that dates to 1612, with an ornate marriage stone symbolising the families of three of the tribes that was discovered when renovations removed the plasterwork to reveal the ancient stonework.

8. TAAFFES BAR

One of Galway's main sports pubs, with a strong affinity to the Gaelic Athletic Association, its walls are adorned with memorabilia celebrating the game's history.

I loved the welcome I received from the Lally family, members of which have run the pub since 1888, and as we supped a couple of pints of Guinness there was the sound of chatter in the Irish language nearby.

Q. LYNCH'S CASTLE

Constructed in the sixteenth century by the influential Lynch family, who were one of the fourteen 'tribes' of Galway, with James (who we met earlier on) acting as the city's mayor.

The castle served as both a family home and a defensive structure, and was constructed to showcase the wealth and high status of its merchant owners.

9. GARAVAN'S BAR

Like many Irish pubs it retains the family name, having been established by Charles Garavan Sr in 1937. Although long gone, its original foundations trace back to 1650, with some of the fireplaces and medieval walls being uncovered during the most recent renovations.

Originally combining a pub with a grocery shop, it has since compiled one of Galway's most extensive whiskey collections, featuring more than 125 varieties. So, it is hardly surprising that my camera assistant, Luke, and I popped back here at the end of the day to try a few drops and an Irish coffee.

R. STATUE OF OSCAR WILDE AND EDUARD VILDE

This eye-catching sculpture features the two esteemed writers seated together on a granite bench, engaged in conversation.

Oscar Wilde was notable for his wit and humour, delivering famous quotes such as 'I have nothing to declare except my genius' at US customs, 'Be yourself; everyone else is already taken', 'We are all in the gutter, but some of us are looking at the stars' and 'To live is the rarest thing in the world. Most people exist, that is all.'

Estonian Eduard Vilde, on the other hand, often focused his works on social justice, class struggles, and the conflicts between traditional and modern values in his country's society.

Despite being of a similar age, the two never actually met, and the sculpture, created in 1999, was installed in Tartu, Estonia, with a replica gifted to Galway in 2004.

10. THE HOLE IN THE WALL

This brightly coloured, thatched building was constructed in the 1870s and originally used as a farming supplies store, with the space behind used for horses and deliveries.

Its name is a source of local legend, and when I was there the staff were unable to shed any more light – but let's not allow the truth to get in the way of a good story, as one tale is as simple as the wall having a hole that enabled off-duty officers to enjoy a pint in the adjoining garda station. An alternative version suggests a more sinister link to smuggling and pirates from medieval times.

S. THE BROWNE DOORWAY

The doorway originally served as the entrance to the Browne family residence on Lower Abbeygate Street – the Brownes being one of Galway's fourteen ruling merchant families. It was constructed in 1627 and includes a Latin inscription from Psalm 127:1 on the architrave, which reads, 'Nisi Dominus aedificaverit domum, in vanum laboraverunt, qui aedificant eam' ('If the Lord does not build a house, then those who build it work in vain').

11. THE SKEFF LATE BAR & KITCHEN

On the edge of the park, this pub is huge as it encompasses six bars spread across five floors.

It is by far the largest in the city and, covering 10,000 square feet, it would have been very impressive in its original use as a stately home before its conversion into the Skeffington Arms in 1850.

Like a lot of Galway pubs, it is very proud of its whiskey collection and, despite being eleven pubs in, not all heroes wear capes and the least I could do was grab a few glasses from the pub's own barrel!

T. EYRE SQUARE

Although officially renamed John F. Kennedy Memorial Park in 1965 – following the former US President's 1963 visit just five months before his assassination – the location is still widely known as Eyre Square.

It was here, at the doorstep of the Browne Doorway, that he

delivered a short speech acknowledging the special connection between Ireland and those Irish people that had emigrated to America, going as far as to quote the Gaelic expression, 'Céad míle fáilte', which literally means 'One hundred thousand welcomes'.

12. O'CONNELL'S BAR

Although it showed them entering this pub through a tiny red door (actually in a building by the Spanish Arch), it was in this pub that Saoirse Ronan and Ed Sheeran were seen dancing in the video for his hit song 'Galway Girl'.

Originally established as a grocery store in 1862, the main bar has retained many of its original fixtures, such as the small bar, tiling, lighting and glasswork, all under an ornate pressed tin ceiling.

Fully converted into a pub in the 1970s, it winds through, past a replica sweet shop, and opens out into a large beer garden, affectionately known as 'Gin Lane' and laid out to resemble a Victorian street.

I absolutely adored the Dough Bros pizzeria at the back of the garden, and it's not surprising as they were voted Ireland's best pizzas and fifteenth in the world at a special competition in Naples.

13. AN PÚCÁN

Almost hidden behind the long bar room is a beer garden, imaginatively known as 'The Garden', which is surprisingly large and often considered one of the best places to watch sport on the big screens.

The venue is reasonably new for the city, having opened in 1985; however, it was transformed by the Connacht Hospitality Group, which also owns the hotel just five minutes from the city where I stayed on my last trip.

There is a huge illuminated sign reading 'GALWAY' in the garden, which was the perfect backdrop to our video of the route – if only we had remembered to switch the microphones on!

LIMERICK
(People's Park to Poems)

Taking in one of the oldest cities in Ireland, this route explores the heart of the city before passing the famous castle and crossing the rapid River Shannon.

It is easy to miss this city on a trip to the island because, despite being just moments from Shannon Airport, it's rare to encounter tourists here.

However, there are few better welcomes than those I received at the Glen Tavern and Mother Macs. And sitting by the water's edge eating shrimp tacos at the Locke Bar is a perfect spot when the sun is shining.

On all the occasions I have visited, I have stayed at the Old Quarter Townhouse, which is a great place to start exploring from.

I particularly enjoyed being a Londoner trying to decipher the accent. When some of the park gardeners poked fun at our filming and said they'd been to London, I couldn't tell if they were laughing or angry at my reply of 'I don't need to know which prison you went to!'

Start at People's Park (V94 NF72).

1. **W.J. South's Bar** *1.00 p.m.*
4 Quinlan Street, V94 A430

2. **Glen Tavern** *1.30 p.m.*
1–2 Lower Glenworth Street, V94 WF63

3. **The White House** *2.15 p.m.*
52 O'Connell Street, V94 NYH9

4. **Tom Collins** *3.00 p.m.*
34 Cecil Street, V94 N5P3

5. **Jerry Flannery's Bar** *3.30 p.m.*
20 Catherine Street, V94 X751

6. **Myles Breen's Bar** *4.15 p.m.*
18 Shannon Street, V94 DXN3

7. **Mother Macs** *5.00 p.m.*
9 High Street, V94 W8XF

8. **Nancy Blake's** *5.45 p.m.*
19 Upper Denmark Street, V94 T284

9. **The Locke Bar** *6.45 p.m.*
3 George's Quay, V94 K8KX

10. **Treaty City Brewery** *7.30 p.m.*
24 & 25 Nicholas Street, V94 EH57

11. **Katie Daly's** *8.15 p.m.*
12 Castle Street, Castle Parade, V94 F7V7

12. **J.J. Bowles** *9.00 p.m.*
8 Thomondgate, Thomond Gate, V94 HK74

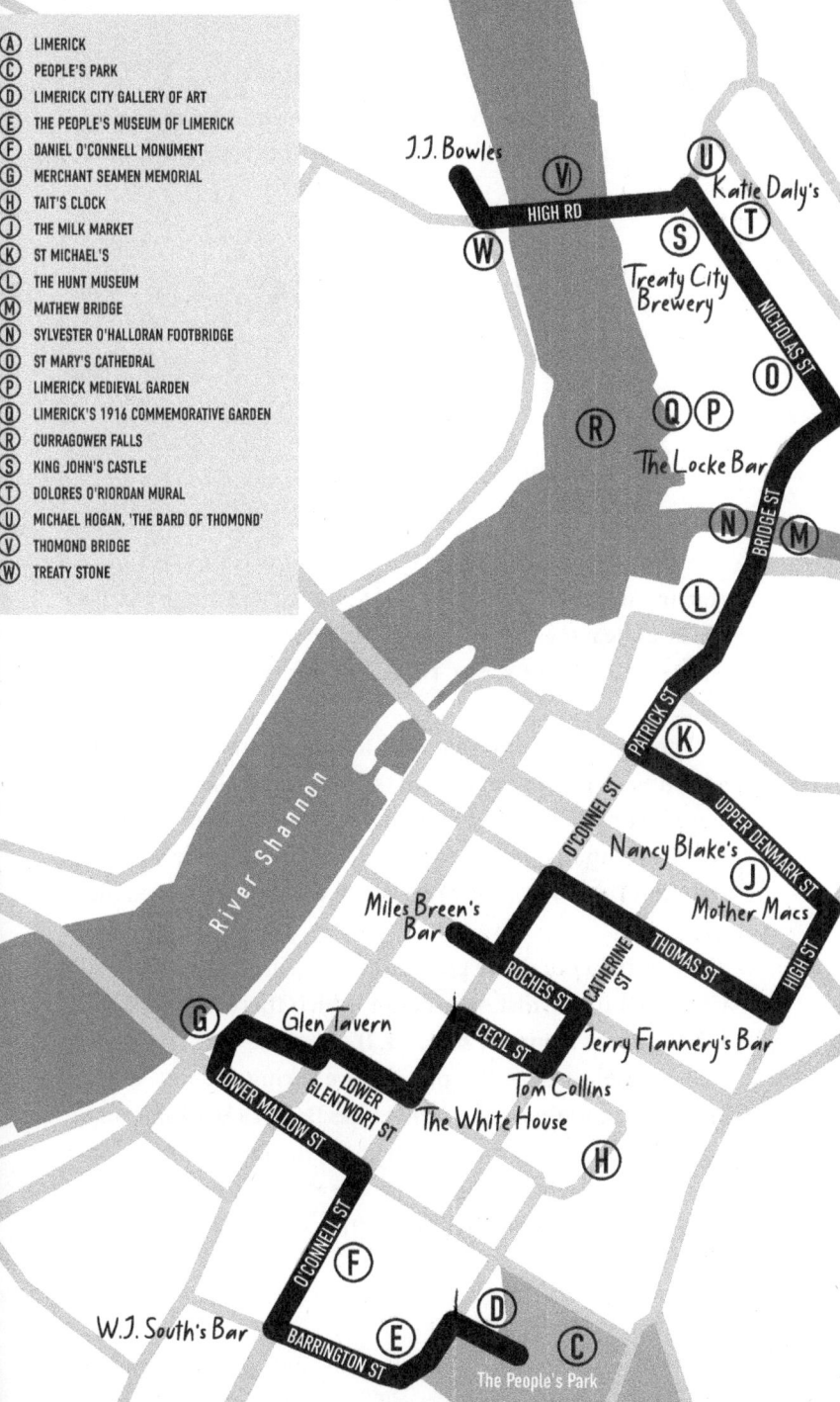

DIRECTIONS

Starting in the heart of the city **(A, B)**, walk through the park **(C, D, E)**, leaving it at the south-west corner, past the church, where **W.J. South's Bar (1)** is on the corner at the main road.

Turn left from the pub and follow the road past Daniel O'Connell's monument **(F)** and take the second left down to the roundabout by the river and the Merchant Seamen Memorial **(G)**. Head up the next road along, taking a quick left/right, to the **Glen Tavern (2)**, with **The White House (3)** the next block along.

Turn right out of the pub, and take the next right with Tait's Clock **(H)** in the distance, before which there is **Tom Collins (4)** and **Jerry Flannery's Bar (5, I)** opposite.

Turn right out of the pub, before taking the first left and crossing the main road, where **Myles Breen's Bar (6)** is on the right. After heading back to the main road, turn left and then take the first right along Thomas Street. At the end of the road turn left and continue before spotting **Mother Macs (7)** at the junction before the Milk Market **(J)**. Just a few yards from the pub is **Nancy Blake's (8)**.

Turn left out of the pub, past the church **(K)**, and at the main road turn right, past the Hunt Museum **(L)**, and head over the bridge **(M, N)** to **The Locke Bar (9)** at the riverside.

Head down the small Merchants Quay, opposite the pub, towards St Mary's Cathedral **(O)**, where there is a view of the waterside **(P, Q, R)**, before following the path right and turning left on Nicholas Street to **Treaty City Brewery (10)**. Leaving the brewery, continue along Nicholas Street, with King John's Castle on your left **(S)**, before **Katie Daly's (11)** just a few yards along the road.

Head past the mural and statue **(T, U)** and cross the river **(V, W)**, taking the first right to **J.J. Bowles (12)**, and start to compose your own limerick **(X)**.

A. LIMERICK

Founded by the Vikings in 922, this ancient city is known as a vibrant cultural hub and the location of King John's Castle, St Mary's Cathedral and Thomond Park – home of the Munster Rugby team that became the first in Irish history to conquer New Zealand's mighty All Blacks.

In literature it was the inspiration for Frank McCourt's novel *Angela's Ashes,* and it is famous for its – usually comedic – 'limerick' poems.

B. LIMERICK (POEM)

Probably the thing that is most associated with the city, but with most people not realising it, this short, five-line comedic poem style follows the specific rhyme scheme AABBA, with the first, second and fifth lines rhyming, as do the third and fourth.

Usually humorous or nonsensical, limericks offer a playful take on their subject matter with the most famous examples coming from Edward Lear, best known for his longer poem, 'The Owl and the Pussycat'.

At the end of the pub crawl I had a go at composing my own version, with the results recorded at the end of this chapter.

C. PEOPLE'S PARK

This nineteenth-century public park in Pery Square marked the start of our day's filming when researching this route.

Opened in 1877, the central bandstand, ornate fountains and traditional bandstand are now lovingly cared for by a team of gardeners, whose banter when we visited was my first experience of the local accent, and to this day I still could not tell you what they said.

D. LIMERICK CITY GALLERY OF ART

At the corner of the square, this gallery was established in 1936 and housed in a Romanesque-style building that was constructed in 1906 as a Carnegie library, funded by the well-known philanthropist.

Born in Dunfermline, Scotland, in 1835, Andrew Carnegie's parents relocated to the United States when he was in his early teens, and he later amassed his fortune leading the expansion of the US steel industry. One of the richest Americans ever to live, in the last eighteen years of his life he donated the equivalent of $10 billion and created more than 2,500 libraries across dozens of countries.

He came under criticism despite his generosity, as his funding covered often elaborate buildings, with local people required to stock and maintain the collections.

When met with criticism from workers as to why the money was not used to increase their wages, Carnegie was said to have quipped, 'If I had raised your wages, you would have spent that money by buying a better cut of meat or more drink for your dinner. But what you needed, though you didn't know it, was my libraries and concert halls.'

Armed with a pint and notes in a makeshift old book before exploring these amazing pubs.

E. THE PEOPLE'S MUSEUM OF LIMERICK

Housed in a Georgian townhouse, this museum showcases local artefacts, photographs and stories from the city's past.

Its most famous exhibit, the Carroll Collection, includes memorabilia dating as far back as the 1700s, including a coat that belonged to Napoleon's older brother, Joseph Bonaparte.

1. W.J. SOUTH'S BAR

Affectionately known by locals simply as South's, this long-established pub has been run by the Hickey family since 1972.

It was originally opened as a pub and general store in 1910 by John Dixon, who married Annie South just two years later.

The wooden interior behind the bar was fitted during the recent refurbishments and the pub has a great reputation for food, with an early breakfast and a hearty lunchtime carvery.

F. DANIEL O'CONNELL MONUMENT

Known as 'The Liberator', this nineteenth-century nationalist leader is best remembered as a campaigner for Catholic emancipation and the repeal of the Act of Union with Britain.

Unveiled in 1857, the monument was the first outdoor public statue of O'Connell in Ireland.

G. MERCHANT SEAMEN MEMORIAL

Original erected as a memorial to local seamen who had lost their lives at sea, it expanded in 2004 to commemorate those who had perished in WWII.

While Ireland was neutral during that war, several merchant vessels were attacked, the most notable being the SS *Kerry Head*, on which twelve died, the SS *Irish Pine*, which was torpedoed, killing thirty-three, and the SS *Clonlara*, which sank on the coast of Portugal, killing eleven.

2. GLEN TAVERN

Established in the 1930s by the Callanan family, the pub is housed in a building dating back to the 1760s.

It was originally three adjacent pubs; however, when the owner of the middle one decided to sell up and incite a bidding war, the two neighbours got together to agree a price themselves, before the winner of a coin toss acquired the property.

I received one of the friendliest welcomes I've had in a pub, as the landlord, Ger, insisted on feeding me and my camera assistant, Luke, with their speciality homemade vegetable soup and fresh bread.

However, while we could have stayed there for quite a while – we can't be stopping when we've got to crawl!

3. THE WHITE HOUSE

As is a theme in the city, this is another pub that claims to be Limerick's oldest, having been established in 1812.

Quite appropriately for such a literary city, this pub hosts the famous White House Poets sessions, which were established by Desmond O'Grady in 1954 and, after a brief hiatus, now host regular readings on the first Wednesday of every month.

H. TAIT'S CLOCK

Erected in 1867, it honours Sir Peter Tait, who despite being born in Scotland, moved to Limerick aged just sixteen and pioneered the use of the Singer sewing machine in Ireland.

He established the city's first clothing factory, which was also one of Europe's first, and become a major supplier to the military – producing more than 120,000 uniforms for the British Army during the Crimean War.

He went on to secure further contracts with the US, before serving three consecutive terms as Limerick's mayor.

Despite his success, he died in poverty after a failed attempt to establish a cigarette factory in Greece after his term in office.

4. TOM COLLINS

Dating to around 1790, this is one of the most distinctive-looking pubs in Limerick, thanks to the red-and-white façade that was added around 1890.

A traditional old pub, it has retained many of its original features and much of the woodwork.

Going back to the 1950s, the pub enjoyed a friendly rivalry with fellow drinking establishment Nancy Blake's, which saw Tom Collins' drinkers taking on their counterparts in an annual inter-pub football match. After a brief absence, the tradition was revived and continued from 2012 when a new owner acquired Nancy Blake's and arranged a contest at nearby Shelbourne Park.

5. JERRY FLANNERY'S BAR

Established in the 1960s by Jerry Flannery Sr, who was a former Munster and Ireland international rugby player, before passing into the hands of his son, also called Jerry Flannery.

It is affectionately known by locals as 'the ball in the wall' due to the large rugby ball bursting through the front.

The building dates to the early 1900s, when it was a whiskey bonder – a company that blends and bottles whiskey rather than doing the actual distilling.

There is a lovely snug at the end of the main bar, which is easy to miss, while to the rear is a huge area that can hold hundreds of people for live music or sporting events. I could not quite believe the size of it when I went to explore back there.

This Limerick landmark is instantly recognisable and has gained cult status in the city.

I. MUNSTER RUGBY TEAM

One of only four professional provincial rugby teams in Ireland, Munster was established in 1879 and is best known for its remarkable victory over the dominant All Blacks.

Playing in the electric atmosphere of Thomond Park, Munster's heroes became the first Irish team ever to beat New Zealand's finest when they ran out 12–0 winners in 1978.

6. MYLES BREEN'S BAR

This rugby bar is a popular spot for fans and has often been voted 'best pub in Limerick'.

While the pub dates to 1802, its current name comes from the owner who acquired it in the 1960s alongside his wife Bridie, and although they left in the 1980s it has retained it.

When I was here, the staff behind the bar were happy to share tales of when Ed Sheeran and his team all piled in after finishing a performance nearby, let the drinks flow and were great company mixing with the locals.

7. MOTHER MACS

A traditional Irish pub, behind Mother Macs' distinctive exterior is a friendly pub that eschews music or sports to encourage conversation.

When I visited, I sat down with Mike McMahon, who has run the pub with his brother James since 2015. He told me the funny tale that he had been on a video call with the city's mayor and, although already in trouble for not attending the meeting in person, politely dropped out of the call to sit with us in the pub's whiskey room and regale us with stories of his time running the pub.

One of the friendliest welcomes in this highly-recommended pub.

J. THE MILK MARKET

This historic covered food market is one of the country's oldest, with roots dating back long before the 1800s.

It was originally known as the corn market, until the scattered nature of the local markets was consolidated here in the 1850s following an act of parliament.

Despite being a key destination for the local population, its operators, the Limerick Market Trustees, experienced severe financial difficulties and went into receivership in 1897. This lasted until 1988, making it the longest period of financial woe in Irish commercial history.

8. NANCY BLAKE'S

Named after the owner who established the pub in 1956, a change was planned following her marriage, but local popularity saw it remain.

To the rear is the popular Outback Bar, which was established when Nancy's son, Donal Mulcahy, took over the pub in 1991 and created a lively music venue.

K. ST MICHAEL'S

The main location for funerals of the city's prominent figures, the most notable being those of former mayor John Daly and Sean South, who was a former IRA member fatally wounded in the New Year's Day attack that took place in Northern Ireland in 1957.

Although originally constructed between 1779 and 1781, the church was rebuilt in 1881 in Italianate and Romanesque Revival styles.

The stone fonts predate the church and, while their origin is unknown, it is believed that they are probably from a chapel that was on this site around 1720.

L. THE HUNT MUSEUM

Named after John and Gertrude Hunt, who established the museum from their personal collection in 1978, when it was relocated here from the University of Limerick.

Over their lifetime, the married historians managed to amass a collection of more than 2,500 artefacts, ranging from prehistoric tools of the Stone Age to modern paintings by artists such as Picasso.

M. MATHEW BRIDGE

A bridge has been on this site since medieval times, with the current version constructed between 1844 and 1846 to replace the previous one from 1762.

It was designed by William Henshaw Owen, who was a notable local architect, and named after Father Theobald Mathew, a prominent temperance reformer who had gathered 180,000 disciples in Limerick by the time the bridge was completed.

N. SYLVESTER O'HALLORAN FOOTBRIDGE

Constructed in 1987, this modern bridge was named in honour of Dr Sylvester O'Halloran, a renowned Limerick-born surgeon and historian.

Born in 1728, O'Halloran is notable for having developed innovative treatments for cataracts – even though it is hard to believe any such method would be available back in the days before sterilisation, antibiotics and painkillers.

9. THE LOCKE BAR

Established in 1724, making it one of Limerick's oldest – a claim several seem to hold – this pub's outside bench seats, overlooking the Abbey River, offer probably the best spot in Limerick to sit on a sunny day.

On my most recent trip, I enjoyed some oysters and shrimp tacos in what claims to be the city's oldest beer garden, but that's a very loose description as we were actually sitting on the aforementioned benches by the riverside.

O. ST MARY'S CATHEDRAL

Founded in 1168, this is the city's oldest continuously used building. Legend claims that the last King of Munster, Domnall Mór Ua Briain, established the cathedral on the site of his palace on King's Island.

The cathedral is notable for housing Ireland's only complete set of medieval misericords – wooden 'ledges' in the cathedral's intricately carved choir stalls, used by monks as a discreet means of support when standing for a long service.

P. LIMERICK MEDIEVAL GARDEN

Originally designed for Ireland's premier garden festival, Bloom 2014, to celebrate Limerick's status as Ireland's first National City of Culture.

The garden showcases medieval gardening techniques, featuring elements such as turf seats, raised beds, gravel paths, and ornamental borders filled with herbs, and edible and medicinal flowers.

It was awarded the silver medal at the exhibition and was seen by over 100,000 visitors.

Q. LIMERICK'S 1916 COMMEMORATIVE GARDEN

Unveiled forty years after the Easter Rising, the project commenced in 1931 but suffered from severe delays due to the outbreak of WWII, and it was not completed until 1956 when James Power, son of the original sculptor, Albert Power, took over following his death.

The memorial features bronze statues of three local figures who played a significant part in the uprising: Tom Clarke, Ned Daly and Con Colbert, all of whom were executed by firing squad.

R. CURRAGOWER FALLS

The River Shannon is Ireland's longest and flows at a remarkable pace. These rapids are especially prominent during low tide, creating a series of cascades and turbulent waters following the construction of a weir to regulate the water levels.

Their name is believed to derive from the Irish 'currach gabhar', which means 'crossing of the goats'.

10. TREATY CITY BREWERY

Originally a passion project (as all the best things are) of Limerick native Stephen Cunneen, the brewery began in Vancouver, Canada, before relocating and setting up here in 2014.

It is housed in two eighteenth-century buildings, of which one was the former residence of three-time Limerick mayor, Arthur Roche, who was notable for running his own brewery from the premises.

I went for a flight of three beers on my visit, although those with more stamina could try up to nine in one sitting.

S. KING JOHN'S CASTLE

Built on what is believed to have been the site of Viking settlements dating to 922, this thirteenth-century fortress was constructed by England's King John around 1200.

It is one of Ireland's best-preserved Norman castles, which is all the more remarkable given that it has endured multiple sieges, most notably in the seventeenth century when it was captured by Irish Confederate forces in 1642.

11. KATIE DALY'S

Originally the site of the Red Lion, which used to serve members of the Crown Forces, the representatives of British authority stationed here before Irish independence.

Today's building was constructed in 1789, although it did not get its current name until it was taken over by Tony and Carol Ryan in 1988, when they renamed it after Tony's grandmother.

T. *DOLORES O'RIORDAN* MURAL

This mural honouring the late Dolores O'Riordan, lead singer of the Cranberries, was unveiled in 2019.

Born in nearby Ballybricken in 1971, the singer was instantly recognisable for delivering her vocals in a strong Limerick accent, and for her signature 'yodelling' style.

Despite achieving international acclaim, she suffered with depression and bipolar disorder throughout her life, which ended in 2018 at the age of just forty-six, when she accidentally drowned in the bath of a London hotel room.

Although not suspicious, the official inquest, which took place about eight months after she died, ruled her death was due to alcohol intoxication.

Do not forget to check on your friends and family. Just because someone is talented and successful does not mean they are not fighting their own battles.

U. MICHAEL HOGAN, 'THE BARD OF THOMOND'

A local legend, who was lauded for his vivid depictions of Limerick's landscapes, history and folklore.

Born in 1828 and educated at the Christian Brothers School, self-taught Irish poet Michael Hogan was said to have penned his first poem at the age of eight.

He was renowned for his satirical writings that critiqued prominent figures in Limerick, often leading to both acclaim and controversy in equal measure.

His most famous poem, the epic *Drunken Thady and the Bishop's Lady*, narrates the tale of a notorious loveable rogue who becomes entangled in a series of absurd situations, generally revolving around a vengeful bishop's wife, and the resulting hilarious clash of classes and social standing.

A good old-fashioned full Irish breakfast is an essential before and after a crawl.

V. THOMOND BRIDGE

The original bridge was said to have been an impressive sight, consisting as it did of fourteen arches, compared to the current version's seven. It was replaced in 1836, with the new bridge incorporating the original's foundations.

W. TREATY STONE

An otherwise unremarkable-looking stone, now raised on a plinth, it was here that the Treaty of Limerick was signed in 1691, effectively ending the Williamite War between the forces of King William III and the Jacobites loyal to the exiled King James II.

The conflict was set against the broader backdrop of the English Revolution, as Ireland became the gateway from which Catholic-supported King James II attempted to wrest control of the British Isles.

Before its association with the treaty, the stone was reportedly used by locals as a block from which to mount horses.

12. J.J. BOWLES

One of the oldest pubs in Limerick, although the Locke claims to be older, the building itself dates to the late 1600s – which means it can claim to be the city's oldest.

It was purchased by Joseph Bowles and his son, J.J., an Irish handball champion, in 1910 after the closure of the nearby Thomondgate Distillery, where Joseph worked.

From its beer garden, it offers a stunning view of King John's Castle.

X. MY LIMERICK

There once was a man with a cheer,
Who wrote of each pub and each beer.
With camera in hand,
He roamed through the land,
Spinning tales that we all love to hear!

CORK
(River to Theatre)

Ireland's second-largest city is often referred to as the 'real capital' by locals, and I loved exploring this medieval area that dates back to around the sixth century.

The accent is a little easier to understand here than some of the others around the island, and I visited on the third consecutive day of pub crawls, with my usual social media video editor, Luke.

There's a real mix of pubs on this route, which tracks the River Lees before winding through the very heart of the city.

I particularly loved the pizza in the beer garden behind the ancient grounds of the Franciscan Well Brewpub, sitting for a stout and whiskey in the highly secretive Hi-B, and speaking with the Cork locals was a real treat – probably one of my very favourite places.

If you're in the mood for dancing, then Crane Lane Theatre is one of the best late-night places I've ever finished a pub crawl in.

Start at Cork (Kent) Station (T23 E6TD).

1. **The Shelbourne Bar** *1.00 p.m.*
17 MacCurtain Street, T23 DE79

2. **Sin É** *1.45 p.m.*
8 Coburg Street, T23 KF5N

3. **Franciscan Well Brewpub** *2.30 p.m.*
14 North Mall, Sunday's Well, T23 P264

4. **Costigan's Pub** *3.15 p.m.*
11 Washington Street West, T12 N768

5. **The Oval** *4.00 p.m.*
25 South Main Street, T12 Y15D

6. **The Vicarstown Bar** *4.45 p.m.*
52 North Main Street, T12 KT92

7. **Rising Sons** *5.30 p.m.*
Cornmarket Street, T12 WK27

8. **Mutton Lane Inn** *6.30 p.m.*
3 St Patrick's Street, Mutton Lane, T12 RV07

9. **The Hi-B** *7.15 p.m.*
108 Oliver Plunkett Street, T12 E6CX

10. **The Long Valley Bar** *8.00 p.m.*
10 Winthrop Street, T12 NW64

11. **Crane Lane Theatre** *9.00 p.m.*
Phoenix Street, T12 A218

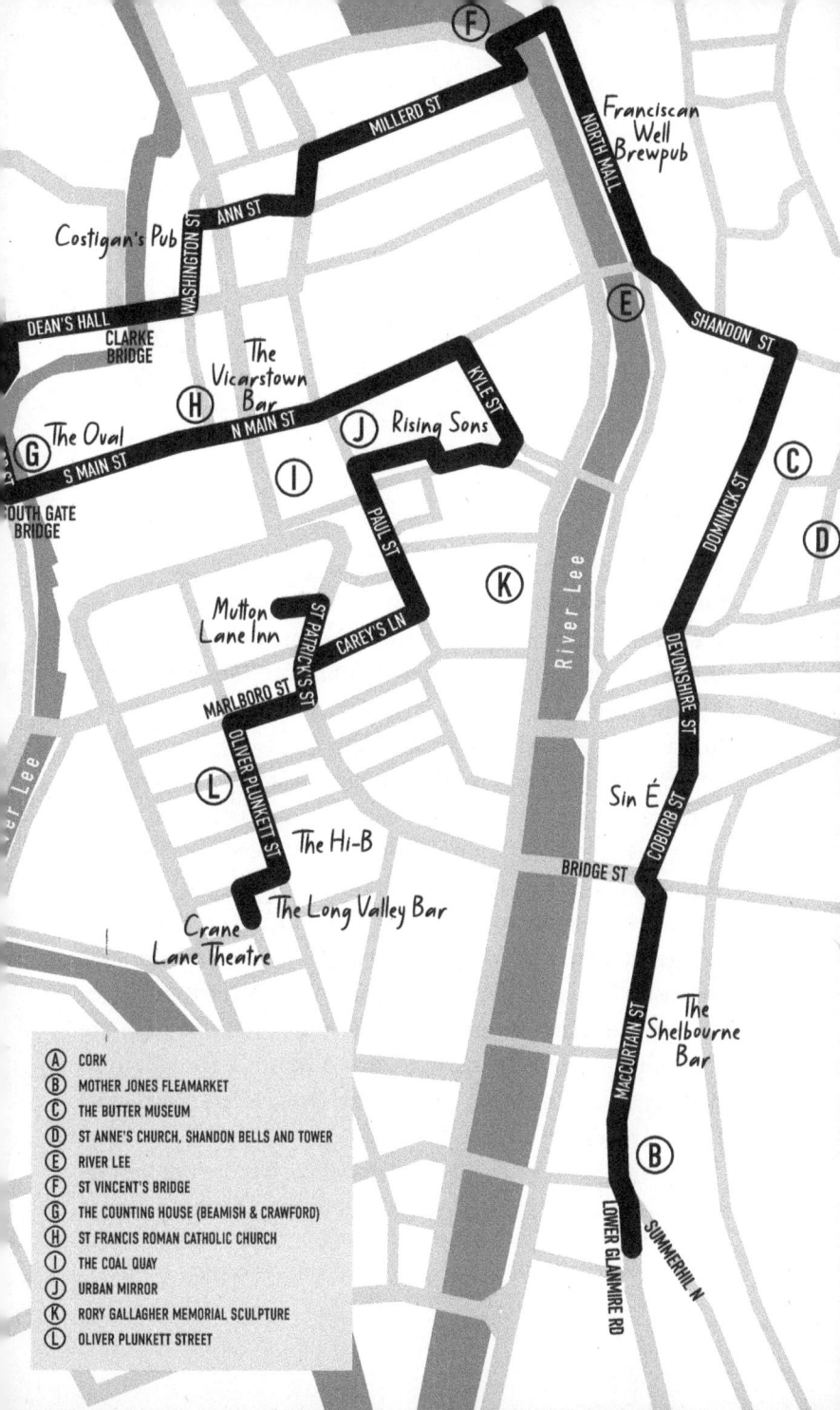

DIRECTIONS

On leaving the station, turn right on Alfred Street, and follow the road as it curves left and joins the main road **(A)**, where the flea market is on the right **(B)** just before **The Shelbourne Bar (1)**. Continue past the pub and go straight over, down the hill, as the road turns left to **Sin É (2)**.

Leaving the pub, continue along the road, crossing the main road, up a narrow street and then up some steps. Continue straight along Dominick Street past the Butter Museum **(C)**, with the church **(D)** in the distance to the right.

At the main road, take a left then turn right before the bridge along the river's edge **(E)**, where the **Franciscan Well Brewpub (3)** is on the right. Leave the pub and cross the river at the pedestrian bridge **(F)**, following the road alongside the river. Cross over at the main road and continue straight until turning left at the other part of the river, where **Costigan's Pub (4)** is further along on the right.

Turn right past the pub and cross the river, before following it left to the next crossing, where the Counting House

(G) is on the left with **The Oval (5)** further along. Continue along this road, where **The Vicarstown Bar (6)** is opposite the church **(H)**.

Take the next right past the pub, into the Coal Quays **(I, J)**, where the **Rising Sons** brewery **(7)** is on the right, along Cornmarket Street.

Turn left at the end of the road and follow the road right, past the church, just before Rory Gallagher's memorial **(K)**. **Mutton Lane Inn (8)** is down an alley on the opposite side of the road.

Return to the main road, taking the second right along Marlboro Street. Turn left onto Oliver Plunkett Street **(L)**, where **The Hi-B (9)** is on the left, with **The Long Valley Bar (10)** around the next corner. Leave the pub and head back towards the main street, before following Pembroke Street opposite, where **Crane Lane Theatre (11)** is down the first left.

A. CORK

Founded as a monastic settlement by St Fin Barre during the sixth century, Cork was a significant trading port for Viking and Norman invaders, and played a major role in the mass emigration during the Great Famine of the 1840s. It is often referred to as the Rebel City, in recognition of its prominent defiance during the Irish War of Independence.

In modern times it has become renowned for its thriving arts scene, excellent food and beautiful surroundings. Some of the landmarks are intimidatingly high on the slopes of the neighbouring hills and my visit reminded me of my time exploring Derry. Thankfully, though, this route sticks very much to the city centre, on and close by the small island where the River Lee divides.

Almost every pub in Ireland has live music.

B. MOTHER JONES FLEA MARKET

This tiny hidden market, squirrelled away in the Victorian Quarter offers an eclectic mix of vintage clothes, books and vinyl. Who knows, maybe an early edition of one of my books will end up there!

1. THE SHELBOURNE BAR

This well-known whiskey bar was established in 1895 and feels a little like being in an old grocery shop, as the worn wooden interior surrounds a low central, island bar.

The bar claims to have the largest collection of Irish whiskeys in the country, with more than 540; however, it is best known for the remarkable achievement of bartender Rory McGee (who coincidentally was born around the corner from where I live in London), who set a Guinness World Record by crafting forty-nine Irish coffees in less than three minutes.

While I would have no chance at that challenge, I did have a go at identifying the different stouts in a flight (three servings of one-third of a pint), where customers are offered Guinness, Murphy's and Beamish to see if they really can tell the difference.

Taste testing Ireland's three most famous stouts – could you tell the difference?

2. SIN É

Pronounced 'shin-ay', its name means 'that's it' in Irish and is a humorous nod to the neighbouring funeral parlour that was present when this tiny pub was established in 1889.

It claims to have the city's longest-running trad music session, with bands performing in one of the bar's corners seven evenings a week.

As well as the knick-knacks and memorabilia on display throughout, it is worth popping upstairs, where there are a couple of barbershop chairs among the jumbled seats and tables.

C. THE BUTTER MUSEUM

Celebrating Ireland's rich butter-making history, this building, which dates to 1849, was pivotal in Cork's rise to the position of largest butter exporter in the world during the nineteenth century.

Although the museum offers visitors the chance to churn their own butter, we've no time for that – we've got pubs to go to.

D. ST ANNE'S CHURCH, SHANDON BELLS AND TOWER

Considered one of the city's most iconic landmarks, it was constructed between 1722 and 1726 and stands on the site of previous churches from medieval times, with the font dating to 1629.

The red sandstone and white limestone of the church's tower are said to represent the salmon of the River Lee.

It is most famous for its eight bells, which weigh more than six tons and were cast in 1750. Visitors can ascend the tower and ring the bells for themselves.

E. RIVER LEE

Travelling from its source in the Shehy Mountains all the way east to Cork Harbour, the river splits in two here, effectively turning the city centre into an island.

This layout has earned Cork the informal title, the Venice of the North, although – having visited the Italian city in the past – I am not sure if there are any other similarities!

3. FRANCISCAN WELL BREWPUB

Although this taproom and brewery was established in 1998, it is on the site of a thirteenth-century Franciscan monastery and its well of the same name.

The original well was rumoured to have healing properties, and was used by the monks to establish their own brewing operations.

I adored sitting in the sun-kissed beer garden, surrounded by the ancient stone walls, and enjoying one of the pub's trademark Pompeii Pizzas, which claim to have won the title 'Ireland's Best' (to be fair, the one I had was incredible).

One of the most popular pizza spots is in the courtyard of this ancient brewery.

F. ST VINCENT'S BRIDGE

This perfect example of Victorian-era engineering was constructed as part of the Cork Improvement Act of 1875 to provide easy passage across the river for the workers from Wyse's Distillery, which was a major employer at the time.

4. COSTIGAN'S PUB

Located on a busy road, the pub has been operating since 1827; however, prior to this it was used as a variety of shops, a fact to which it pays homage throughout.

Originally two buildings, with 10 Washington Street operating as a fishmonger, while number 11 served as a pub, over the years the premises underwent various transformations, including periods as a grocer, boot maker, and even a flour and meal store.

Upstairs, Grannie's Room offers an intimate setting for private gatherings, while the heated beer garden provides a relaxed outdoor space.

I loved perching over the old shop counter for a pint on my visit, and it reminded me of the many pubs I have been to in Ireland that create what is almost a small village in their beer gardens – this being the first I had come across to do the same, but inside the pub.

G. THE COUNTING HOUSE (BEAMISH & CRAWFORD)

This modern mock-Tudor building was constructed in 1919 as part of the Beamish & Crawford brewery complex, and served as the brewery's office headquarters.

The stout itself dates from 1792, when William Beamish and William Crawford established a brewery on the site of St Francis Abbey in Cork.

After quickly becoming one of the largest breweries in Ireland, by the early 1800s it was producing over 100,000 barrels each year, making it one of the largest in the world.

Over the years, the superior marketing clout of Guinness saw its smooth, slightly sweeter taste, compared to Beamish's dry-roasted, bitter flavour, take a vice-like grip on the stout market.

5. THE OVAL

Getting its name from its unusual oval-shaped ceiling, this pub was established in 1759 and was a convenient place for workers at the Beamish & Crawford brewery opposite to stay for the night if they were from out of town.

It was designed by the same firm responsible for the brewery, and is the only pub to appear on the city's list of buildings of significant historical interest.

There are plenty of tales of workers sneakily rolling kegs over the road and into the pub, and some say that they produced their own stout with a remarkably similar flavour.

There is also the legend of a diminutive landlady, who would storm through the pub with a cane to whip drinkers who were lingering too long at last orders.

6. THE VICARSTOWN BAR

This long, narrow bar, which gets its name from an area north of the city, holds a surprise because although the beautiful beer garden is surrounded by centuries-old walls, it is the bizarre mural of hip-hop and rap legends that adorns the inside of the pub that is most striking.

The question is . . . can you name all the famous faces?

H. ST FRANCIS ROMAN CATHOLIC CHURCH

Designed in the Byzantine style, this church was consecrated in 1953 after the previous structure was ruled structurally unsound.

It sits on the location of a former Franciscan place of worship.

I. THE COAL QUAY

It is hard to believe, as you walk past some of the wonky and derelict buildings, that this used to be one of Cork's primary market streets.

Now named after the main type of goods offloaded here, it has also been known as the Timber Quay and the Potato Quay.

Although boats are no longer able to access the area, there are still some traders present who wear the traditional black shawls and are known by the nickname 'Shawlies'.

J. *URBAN MIRROR*

Part of Cork's temporary Urban Sculpture Trail, launched in 2023 and due to run for five years. The trail consists of five contemporary artworks by both Irish and international artists, in this case plattenbaustudio, who are Irish architects now based in Berlin.

The other sculptures on the route are *Sentinels*, featuring stylised seagulls on neon strips, *The Face Cup*, taking inspiration from Bronze Age artefacts, *Boom Nouveau*, which is a 'cultured lamppost', and *Tempus Futurum*, which is projected onto the Triskel Christchurch.

7. RISING SONS

This microbrewery was established in 2014 and its beers can be found in most pubs across the city.

When I visited, they were particularly keen for me to sample their Changeling Pale Ale, which was awarded 'best pale ale in the world up to 5%' at the International Beer Challenge in 2018, having taken the all-Ireland title the year before.

It is notable for using a variety of hops to provide slight variations in flavour, noticeable even when trying it in different Cork pubs, which I was more than happy to attempt. As you know, not all heroes wear capes.

K. RORY GALLAGHER MEMORIAL SCULPTURE

This tribute to legendary Irish rock and blues guitarist, Rory Gallagher, was installed in 1997 during the Cork Jazz Festival.

Constructed from bronze, it represents his guitar intertwined with lyrics from his 1982 album, *Jinx*.

Widely regarded as one of the greatest and most influential guitarists of all time, the self-taught musician refused to conform to commercial pressures, often rejecting record label demands for singles and music videos. His dedication to authenticity made him a cult hero among rock and blues fans.

Jimi Hendrix was once asked how it felt to be the world's best guitarist. He allegedly responded: 'I don't know, ask Rory Gallagher.'

8. MUTTON LANE INN

Hidden down a tiny alley, it is hard to believe that its name comes from its use as a passageway by farmers herding sheep to the English market nearby.

The pub was established in the eighteenth century and its wonky walls and low ceilings are in striking contrast to the vibrant artwork that adorns the alleyway in front of the pub. Known as 'The Pana Shuffle', it was painted in 2004 by local artist Anthony Ruby ahead of Cork's tenure as European City of Culture the following year.

Throughout the artwork are depictions of Cork life, including various real-life traders, street performers and members of the artist's own family. As well as the picture of JFK hanging above the bar inside the pub, Ruby's artwork outside contains a hidden dedication to 'everyone except George Bush'.

L. OLIVER PLUNKETT STREET

A main shopping street, filled with the city's retail outlets and coffee shops, it is named after the Irish Catholic archbishop and martyr who lived from 1625 to 1681.

During his lifetime, many anti-Catholic laws were passed by the English and, although he was a campaigner for Catholic rights, he was falsely accused of treason during the Popish Plot conspiracy – an event invented to cause unrest by falsely accusing Catholics of planning to assassinate the English King Charles II.

After his arrest, Plunkett was hanged, drawn and quartered in London, and it wasn't until 1975 that he became Ireland's first canonised saint in nearly seven hundred years.

Rather gruesomely, his head is preserved in St Peter's Church, Drogheda, as a relic of his martyrdom.

9. THE HI-B

Officially known as the Hibernian Bar, this tiny venue was established in 1923 and was one of the pubs in Ireland I was most looking forward to visiting.

Housed in the upper floor of the former Hibernian Hotel, the bar's former owner, Brian O'Donnell, was notorious for his disdain for mobile phones, first banning them and then occasionally going so far as to either eject drinkers caught using them, or snatch their phones and cast them through an open window to the street below.

Patrons are encouraged to share tables or sit at the semi-circular bar and sample the establishment's famous whiskey. I was lucky enough to get the chance to sit down and interview one of the team, and was privileged to film the interior for my social media – a true first!

Notoriously secretive, it was a rare privilege to get a photo of Luke sampling the whiskey collection.

10. THE LONG VALLEY BAR

This was one of the most mentioned pubs along the route, so I admit to initially feeling a little underwhelmed when I walked in to this family-run pub, which was established in 1842.

Built on the site of a former stable for the Post Office, the pub was taken over in 1927 by John Moynihan.

Once I had noticed it, it was impossible to ignore that the interior of this pub, with its long, polished bar, is fitted out with parts of an old ship. There was a bunch of friendly chaps sitting in the snug at the front, next to the etched-glass doors taken from White Star liner RMS *Celtic*, which ran aground in Cork Harbour during 1928.

The pub has a proud reputation for its award-winning sandwiches, and still displays certificates from its victories over previous years.

11. CRANE LANE THEATRE

This renowned live music venue and bar has become a cornerstone of the local late-night scene and is the perfect place to conclude our crawl.

Housed down an illuminated alley, in the remnants of an old gentlemen's club that dates to the 1920s, the venue is a mix of bars, dance floors and stages.

As the pub expanded it absorbed the adjacent pharmacy, but rather than clear out the rooms, it retained many of the old products in glass cabinets, and has transformed the place into a fancy cocktail bar, where my host, Kate, helped me sample my way through the selections!

Part of the Crane Lane complex includes this fancy cocktail bar where our host Kate joined me for the day's final drink.

KINSALE
(Fort to The Market)

It is hard to fathom how this little town, with its pretty coloured houses, pinned between two ancient forts, has produced such a storied past.

Alongside the tales of military sieges and brazen love affairs, the joviality of Keith Floyd's boozy breakfasts and its being the birthplace of the first human to exceed 8 feet tall, the town also boasts some of the most beautiful pubs in Ireland.

The walk to and from the first pub can feel like hard work on a sunny day, but it is well worth it for the view over the harbour and pretty town. It's the only significant walk of the route as there is otherwise a pub almost every other building.

As is the case with a lot of Irish pubs, the staff enjoy one another's establishments, and I bumped into the same faces several times along the route.

This is without doubt one of the most picturesque towns in Ireland, and when the sun is shining it is absolutely glorious.

Start at the Bulman Bar & Restaurant in Summercove (PF17 KF57).

12. **The Bulman Bar & Restaurant** *1.30 p.m.*
Summercove, PF17 KF57

13. **The Spaniard** *2.30 p.m.*
Scilly, P17 Y156

14. **Hamlets Bar & Kitchen** *3.30 p.m.*
The Glen, P17 R722

15. **Sam's Bar** *4.00 p.m.*
4 The Glen, P17 AP90

16. **The Fifth Ward Bar** *4.30 p.m.*
The White House, P17 Y504

17. **Kitty Ó Sé's** *5.00 p.m.*
1 Pearse Street, P17 DR67

18. **Dalton's Bar** *5.30 p.m.*
3A Market Street, P17 E068

19. **The Grey Hound/The Market Bar** *6.15 p.m.*
Market Square, P17 PV44

20. **The Tap Tavern** *7.00 p.m.*
Guardwell, P17 AF50

21. **The Lord Kingsale** *7.45 p.m.*
4 Main Street, P17 AX67

22. **Oscar Madisons** *8.30 p.m.*
7 Main Street, P17 RX85

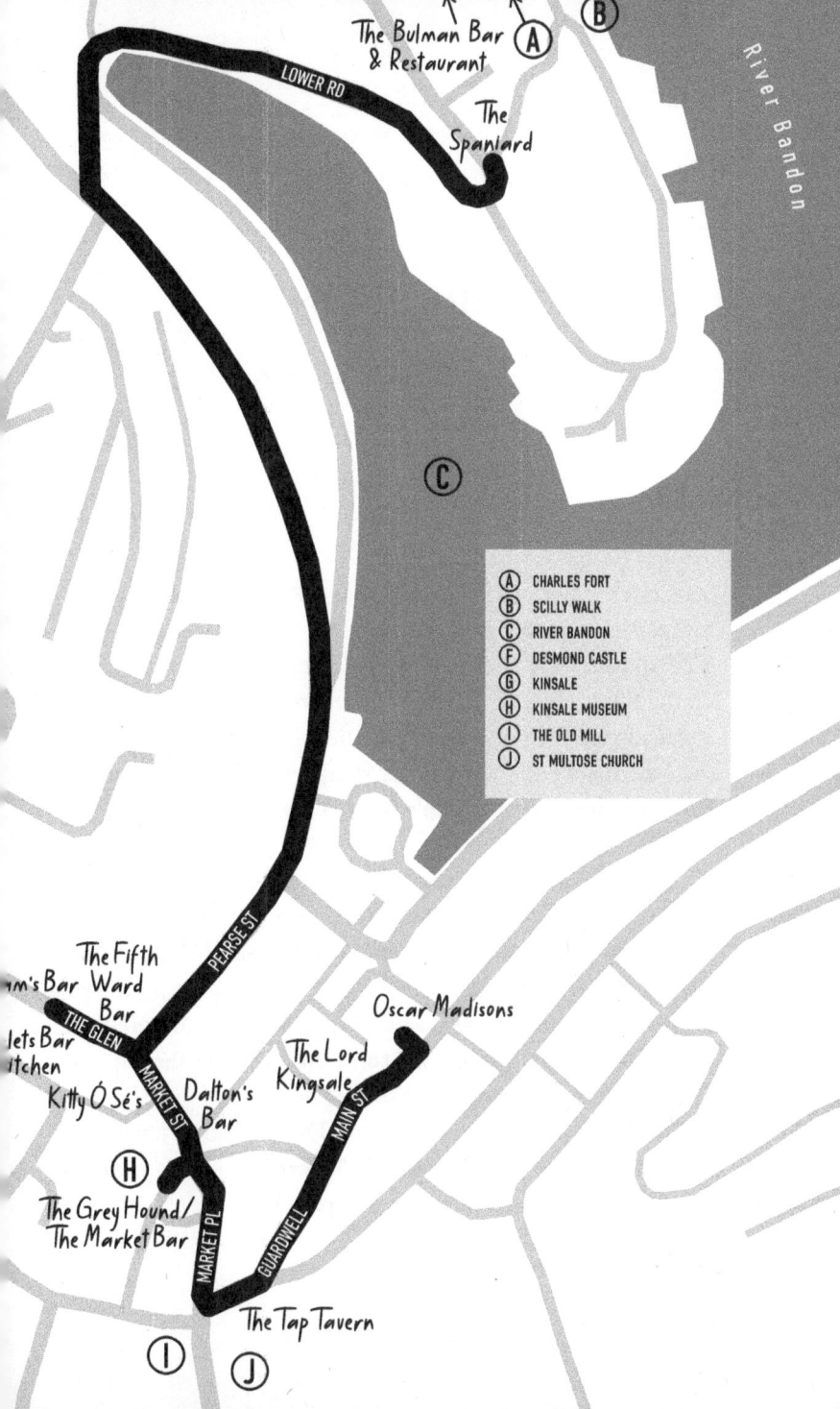

DIRECTIONS

Start out of town at **The Bulman Bar & Restaurant (1)**, opposite Charles Fort **(A)**. Head along Scilly Walk **(B)**, where there is a fantastic view of the bay **(C, D)** as it loops round and back up the hill to the bright-yellow **Spaniard (2, E)**.

Head past the pub and follow the loop of the road around the bay, before the road turns sharp right, where **Hamlets Bar & Kitchen (3)** and **Sam's Bar (4)** are almost next to each other.

Turn left out of the pub, where Desmond Castle **(F)** is a couple of roads away, and head back towards the town centre, where **The Fifth Ward Bar (5)** and **Kitty Ó Sé's (6)** are within a few yards of each other.

Leave the pub to the rear and turn left into the prettiest part of Kinsale **(G)**, where **Dalton's Bar (7)** is on the left and **The Grey Hound/Market Bar (8)** opposite.

Head up Market Place (not Lane, Quay or Street), past the Kinsale Museum **(H)**, to **The Tap Tavern (9)** just in front of the Old Mill **(I)** and St Multose Church **(J)**.

Head down the road, where **The Lord Kingsale (10)** is on the left just before **Oscar Madisons (11)**.

---

1. THE BULMAN BAR & RESTAURANT

The current pub dates to at least the early 1800s, although there is some evidence of a public house serving the nearby fort as far back as the early seventeenth century.

It was originally named the Thatch before adopting the name Barry's from the family who took it over at the turn of the twentieth century.

The current name comes from a navigational buoy called the Bulman, which in turn was named after a rogue vessel that strayed into the waters unannounced.

On my visit, I enjoyed taking my glass out to the beach in front of the pub and paddling in the cool waters while holding my pint.

A. CHARLES FORT

One of Ireland's best-preserved star-shaped military fortifications, it was constructed between 1670 and 1682 to protect the harbour during the reign of King Charles II.

The angled walls are designed to deflect cannon fire, and it was built on the site of an earlier stronghold used during the siege of Kinsale in 1601.

Fast-forward to more recent times and its importance

declined in the twentieth century, which saw it deliberately burned and ruined during the Irish Civil War in 1922.

Most famously, legends tell that Charles Fort is haunted by the ghost of the White Lady – a grieving new bride who flung herself from its ramparts after the death of her husband, mistakenly shot by her own father.

It is claimed that her spirit still wanders the grounds to this day. Luckily, this route starts near the fort during daylight hours.

B. SCILLY WALK

This lovely coastal walk offers a great view of the town and involves only a gentle elevation between the village of Summercove and our next pub.

It is unrelated to the 1970s Monty Python sketch, which tells the tale of Mr Teabag of the Ministry of Silly Walks (played by John Cleese), whose absurd walking and pomposity pokes fun at the bureaucracy and inefficiency of government departments.

While it might be amusing to attempt your own silly walk along this route, it's probably best avoided on a sunny day, as we definitely needed a drink on reaching the next pub.

Despite squinting with a hangover, it was wonderful that the sun was shining during the walk into the centre of Kinsale.

C. RIVER BANDON

Flowing from the Shehy Mountains, this tidal river has provided the backbone to the town's trade for hundreds of years, with its estuary becoming a royal dockyard for ship repair in the seventeenth century.

D. RMS *LUSITANIA*

Tragically, this vessel – the world's largest and fastest passenger liner at the time of its construction – was torpedoed by a German U-boat on 7 May 1915, 11 miles off the Old Head of Kinsale, during what would have been its final voyage.

Almost 1,200 lives were lost in what was the catalyst for rising public support encouraging the United States to enter WWI. Local fishermen rushed to recover survivors among the wreckage.

2. THE SPANIARD

With its location on a spur into the river, it is believed that the site once hosted a seventeenth-century fort or castle.

The stunning mural on its side, distinctive yellow paint and uneven floors under low ceilings make it one of the most famous pubs in Ireland.

Its name comes from Don Juan del Águila, who was the Spanish General during the siege of Kinsale in 1601.

The Spanish reinforced the Irish fighters, against the Protestant English, during the Nine Years' War, with more than 3,500 troops. Despite reinforcements arriving from the north, the English forces exceeded 12,000 troops, leading to a Spanish retreat and crushing Irish defeat that led to the end of the war and more direct English control throughout Gaelic Ireland.

E. KEITH FLOYD

The larger-than-life celebrity chef of BBC fame spent several years here, embracing the coastal town's laid-back rhythms and seafood-rich cuisine.

Although his life was often chaotic – battling bankruptcy and celebrity life in the mid-1990s – he settled in the tranquillity of Creek Cottage on Belgooly Creek, which was a waterside retreat that he transformed from a humble cottage into a bohemian homestead complete with gardens, a boathouse, pigpen, chicken coop and barbecue pits.

Still referred as 'Floyds', it was the perfect place for his legendary wine-fuelled parties. He spent most of his final years in France, returning to England shortly before his death in 2009.

3. HAMLETS BAR & KITCHEN

Part of the Blue Haven Hotel, which dates back to the 1800s when it would have originally served as the town's fish and meat market as well as a warehouse.

I almost missed this place on the route, until we passed the side gate and were drawn in by the pretty row of painted houses in the beer garden, the far end of which, past the polar bear, sits hard up against the rock walls.

4. SAM'S BAR

Acquired by a man called Sam, who lent the pub the name it bears today, it was run by the Murphy family, and the snug that is now filled with Isle of Man TT memorabilia would have often hosted grieving families who had come to make arrangements at the next-door undertakers.

These days, the staff still have to jump from behind the bar to close the curtains and door as a mark of respect when a funeral procession passes.

F. DESMOND CASTLE

A key location for Kinsale's bustling trade, its roots date back as far as 1500, when Maurice FitzGerald, the ninth Earl of Desmond, erected a fortified customs house to collect tariffs and taxes on imported goods.

It evolved into a powder magazine for the occupying forces during the 1601 siege and, following the end of the war, the building was used as a naval prison, where French, Spanish, Portuguese, Dutch and even American prisoners of war were held.

The squalid conditions and overcrowding gave it a notorious reputation, until a 1747 fire claimed the lives of more than fifty inmates, with the building slowly falling into neglect over the next 250 years.

In 1997 it was restored and transformed into Ireland's International Museum of Wine, although legends and tales of the supernatural cries and moans of the fire's victims still abound.

5. THE FIFTH WARD BAR

Formerly White House Bar, as part of the White House Guesthouse, it was renamed in 2018 to celebrate Kinsale's relationship with sister city Newport in Rhode Island, USA.

The current name references the mostly Irish neighbourhood in Newport, where immigrants settled in the 1820s.

The bar features a memorial wall to those who lost their lives in the events of the 9/11 World Trade Center attacks, and includes parts of the buildings and an original firefighter's uniform.

6. KITTY Ó SÉ'S

Named after the aristocratic granddaughter of the Lord Mayor of London, who is best known for her scandalous romance with the charismatic leader of the Irish Home Rule movement, Charles Stewart Parnell.

Born in Essex, Katharine was twenty-two when she married Captain William H. O'Shea of the British Army's 18th Hussars, before the marriage deteriorated in 1875.

Her affair with Parnell started around 1880 and led to the birth of three children, with her husband said to have tolerated this for the sake of his own political or financial gain.

Kitty's public profile was elevated throughout this time, mainly due to the wealth she was expected to inherit from her aunt – until it went elsewhere in 1889, leading her husband to file for divorce, with the subsequent split causing a scandal that devastated Parnell's political career.

G. KINSALE

Its name comes from the Gaelic Ceann tSaile, which means 'head of the sea', and this pretty port town developed from a fishing village, dating as far back as the twelfth century.

Its harbour has been used as a strategic location for both Spanish and English fleets, with the battle, or siege, of Kinsale in 1601 being one of the defining moments of Irish history, leading as it did to the collapse of Gaelic resistance.

In recent times its gorgeous painted buildings and award-winning restaurants have seen it become a popular destination, particularly with American tourists.

One of the prettiest towns in the world, the vibrant colours of its buildings are breathtaking.

7. DALTON'S BAR

Opened in the 1970s by the family of the same name, its current owner, Colm, pays tribute to his late uncle John McNally with a picture of the man who was the first Irish boxer to win an Olympic medal when he was awarded Silver at the 1952 Helsinki Games.

Colm was on a pub crawl of his own the day we visited, and we bumped into him and his pals a few times along the route – proof that the local owners and staff are quite happy supporting one another's pubs.

8. THE GREY HOUND/THE MARKET BAR

Claiming the title of the town's oldest licensed premises, the Grey Hound is said to date from 1690. The surrounding area is built on reclaimed land, so it would originally have sat closer to the water's edge and been a popular destination for sailors, merchants and the fishermen who moored their vessels next to the pub.

Its beer garden contains an ancient stone-lined well, tossing a coin into which, legend claims, will grant safe passage across the seas. Perhaps, at this point in the crawl, it is worth just wishing for safe passage across the next few pubs.

The Grey Hound and our next venue, the Market Bar, are counted as one pub for the purposes of this crawl – the two buildings are joined together, so it is possible to order a pint in one and walk through to the other.

The stones of the Market Bar building are claimed to have been laid a long time before it was granted its licence in the late seventeenth century.

Legend tells of a visiting fiddler who started playing just before closing, leading to everyone lingering, as the drinks flowed, until dawn.

H. KINSALE MUSEUM

Housed in the old town's market house, this handsome seventeenth-century building once served as the courthouse and civic hub for the area.

It was restored and reopened in 1993 to house artefacts from the 1601 siege, the sinking of the *Lusitania* and many other nautical remnants dating back hundreds of years.

Most curious is an enormous pair of boots once worn by Patrick Cotter O'Brien, who was born nearby and grew to be one of the tallest humans of all time. In fact, if you have followed the routes in my England book you may well have stood in the same spot he did, outside a York pub.

Cotter was the first human verified at over 8 feet tall, who after breaking with his promoter, a showman who, after breaking with his promoter – a showman who had displayed him in exhibitions across England – went on to run his own attraction, charging a reduced rate for the working classes.

Having originally started work as a humble bricklayer and plasterer, on his death he left £2,000 to his mother – a fortune at the time.

9. THE TAP TAVERN

Opened in 1886, its beer garden has a deep, ancient well that dates to the 1100s, from which locals used to collect natural spring water, demonstrating the reason for the original name of the area, Fan na dTubraid ('slope of the springs').

What started out with one gift from an American tourist now sees all fifty US states represented by vehicle number plates pinned to the walls and ceilings.

Landlady Mary is pictured on the walls too, meeting the Duchess of York, Sarah Ferguson, who visited back when she was horse riding nearby. Also featured is retired NASA astronaut Dan Tani, who is connected to the pub through his Cork-born wife. Having first travelled into space on the *Endeavour* in 2001, he spent a further 131 days on the International Space Station between 2007 and 2008.

I. THE OLD MILL

More formally known as the James O'Neill Building, there has been a structure on this site for at least the last four hundred years.

A smaller mill and starch works was established in the early 1820s beside Belgooly Creek, but by 1832 a much larger six-storey flour mill needed to be built.

It operated for around thirty years before it was converted into a whiskey distillery in 1872. Over time it fell into disuse, even surviving attempts to demolish it with explosives in 1941.

By the late twentieth century local campaigners had begun preservation efforts to restore what was now a hollow stone shell, and in December 2023 it reopened as Kinsale Library.

J. ST MULTOSE CHURCH

One of Ireland's oldest continuously used churches, it was built around 1190 on the site of an even earlier church from the sixth century.

Over the years it has been greatly developed, with the addition of a Norman bell tower in the twelfth century, and further decorative and structural enhancements in the mid-

1700s and later between 1835 and 1856.

As news of the execution of King Charles I reached the town in 1649, the then Prince Rupert declared the new king within its walls.

Inside the church look out for the clasped hands, carved out of stone, that have been worn down by the fishermen's wives who were said to rub them for luck before their husbands set off out to sea.

The graveyard is the final resting place of some of the victims of the *Lusitania* sinking in 1915.

10. THE LORD KINGSALE

One of the town's oldest, this is the pub that most locals recommended to me along the route as their favourite.

Although its exact date of construction is unknown, it is one of many buildings in the area that were owned by the coastguard before it was purchased and converted into a pub, first called Cotters.

The current name comes from an ancient Irish peerage, which originated around 1223 under King Henry III, making it one of Ireland's oldest.

I love the chance to meet social media followers and here Chris joined me for a pint of plain.

11. OSCAR MADISONS

Another pub that was converted from a former coastguard building, its name is a playful nod to the sportswriter character made famous by Walter Matthau in the 1968 film *The Odd Couple*.

It has a reputation as a popular sports place, and its late-night licence made it the perfect spot for us to finish the day's filming.

The Wild Atlantic Way ensures that Ireland is one of the best places to eat seafood like this giant oyster.

WATERFORD
(Bridge to the Ships)

Ireland's oldest city can appear quite industrial on the approach over the river; however, when the sun shines on the old buildings its medieval heritage starts to show.

The route starts along the river, before winding through the traditional market squares and the cultural hub of the city.

Famous for its glasswork, the museum quarter features ancient towers, imposing churches and modern buildings housing some of Ireland's most famous artefacts.

Among the pubs is the iconic J. & K. Walsh, which would be one of the most interesting on any route, as it steps back in time to a day when pubs mixed their purpose with the local shops of years gone by.

I particularly loved the music throughout the pubs, and we returned to An Uisce Beatha at the end of the day to hear more, before retiring to our rooms at the historic four-star Granville Hotel.

Start at the Rice Bridge (Waterford, R680).

1. **Grattan Bar** *1.30 p.m.*
1 & 2 Bridge Street, X91 YD52

2. **An Uisce Beatha** *2.00 p.m.*
8 Merchants Quay, X91 PR27

3. **Tully's Bar** *2.45 p.m.*
37 O'Connell Street, X91 AY62

4. **Thomas Maher** *3.30 p.m.*
20 O'Connell Street, X91 HR22

5. **J. & K. Walsh Victorian Spirit Grocer** *4.15 p.m.*
11 Great George's Street, X91 VH93

6. **The Gingerman** *5.00 p.m.*
6 Arundel Lane, X91 X327

7. **The Hub** *5.45 p.m.*
27 Michael Street, X91 DK84

8. **Geoff's Café Bar** *6.30 p.m.*
9 John Street, X91 WP98

9. **Davy Macs** *7.15 p.m.*
John's Avenue, X91 V3YR

10. **Jordan's Bar** *8.00 p.m.*
123 Parade Quay, X91 CP89

11. **Katty Barry's** *8.30 p.m.*
2 Mall Lane, X91 EA38

12. **The Three Shippes** *9.00 p.m.*
18 William Street, X91 KX20

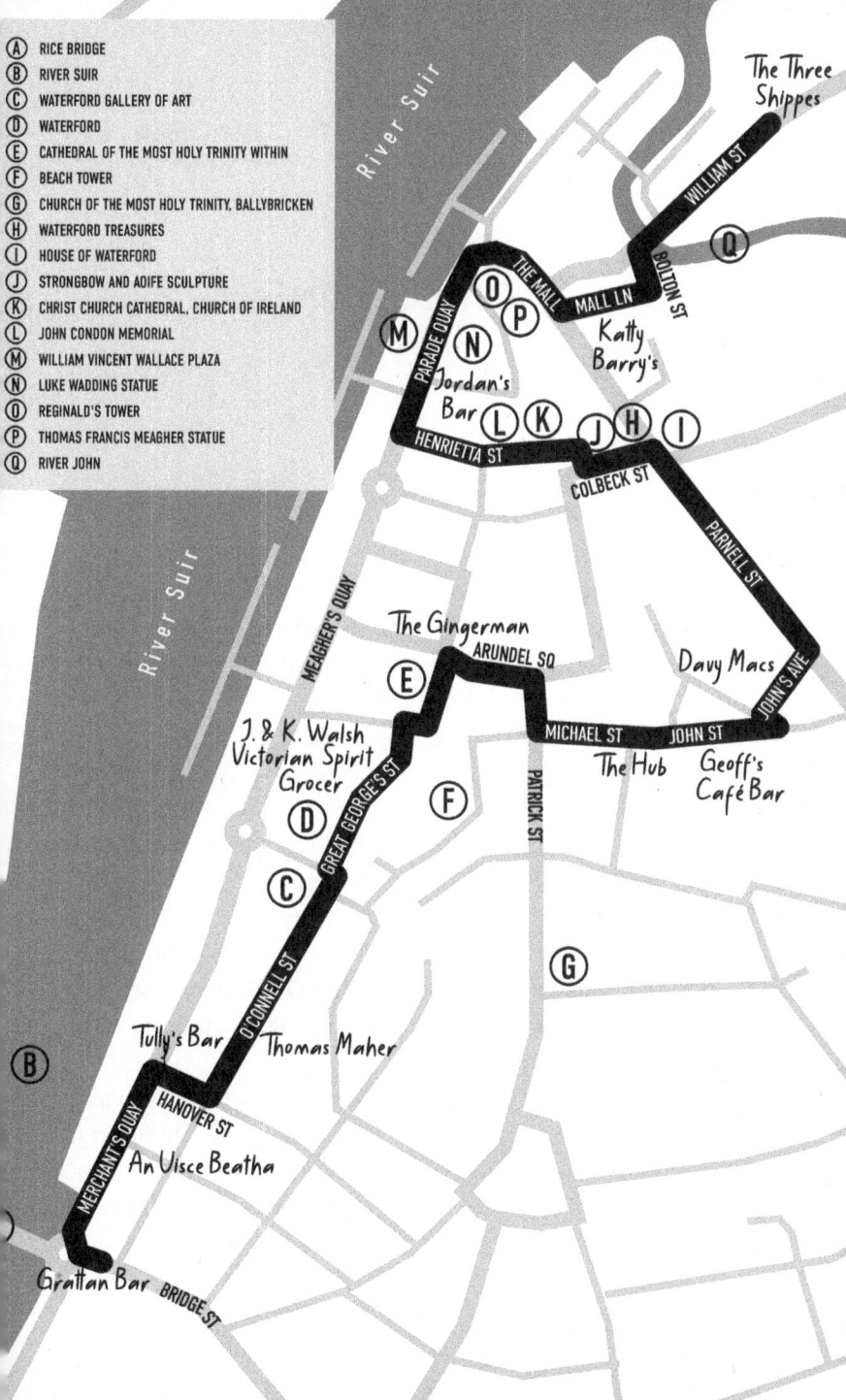

DIRECTIONS

Start at **Grattan Bar (1)** opposite the Rice Bridge **(A)** before continuing along the River Suir **(B)**, where **An Uisce Beatha (2)** is on the right. Continue past the pub before turning right up Hanover Street and left at the crossroads, where **Tully's Bar (3)** is opposite **Thomas Maher (4)**.

Exit the pub past the Waterford Gallery of Art **(C)** and continue to **J. & K. Walsh (5)**. At the end of the pedestrian area **(D)**, with the church on the left **(E)**, **The Gingerman (6)** is a few steps away, through the market square.

Head back to the square, taking a detour straight ahead to Beach Tower **(F)** and the Cathedral of the Most Holy Trinity **(G)**, or turn left and head to **The Hub (7)** on the corner, with **Geoff's Café Bar (8)** further along and **Davy Macs (9)** down the tiny alleyway opposite.

Turn left at the end of the main road and continue until turning first left past Waterford Treasures and other sites of the medieval quarter **(H, I, J, K, L, M, N)**.

Follow the road as it curves right, before emerging at the

water, where **Jordan's Bar (10)** is close to Reginald's Tower **(O)**.

Continue along the road **(P)** and cross onto Mall Lane with **Katty Barry's (11)** on the left.

Emerge at the end of the road to cross the river **(Q)** and continue to the final pub, **The Three Shippes (12)**.

---

1. GRATTAN BAR

Named after the Irish politician behind the securing of legislative independence for Ireland in 1782, the pub is believed to have opened around the turn of the twentieth century.

It was Henry Grattan's campaigning that pushed the British government to grant greater rights to the Irish movement, creating what was affectionately known as 'Grattan's Parliament'.

When the Act of Union was passed in 1800, he took his seat in the British House of Commons, which he held until his death in 1820. He was buried in Westminster Abbey alongside British prime ministers.

A curious quirk of this pub is that when it was taken over in November 2013 the new owner erected Christmas trees, which remain to this day and are rebranded as 'occasional trees' depending on the season.

A. RICE BRIDGE

With the official name Brother Edmund Ignatius Rice Bridge, it is easy to see why it's usually referred to by its shortened form.

Replacing the earlier Redmond Bridge, it was constructed between 1982 and 1986, with the first two of its four lanes opening to vehicles in October 1984.

It is named after the Waterford-born founder of the Christian Brothers, who arrived in 1779, when the absence of a bridge would have seen ferries cross here, carrying passengers into the city centre.

B. RIVER SUIR

Winding for more than 110 miles from the slopes of Devil's Bit Mountain, this river has been recognised since the time of the Vikings, since when it has been important in the transporting of fish, timber and other produce inland.

The river is famous for its salmon and brown trout, with a record catch, landed in 1874, of a salmon weighing an incredible 57 pounds (a fraction over 4 stone).

2. AN UISCE BEATHA

This pub's name is an original Gaelic term, meaning 'water of life', that first appeared in early Irish monastic writings as a translation of the Latin *aqua vitae*.

It referred to the distilled alcohol that was used for medicinal and ritual purposes between the sixth and twelfth centuries. It is hard to believe now, but as the words changed over the centuries this became the foundation for the modern words 'whiskey' in Ireland and 'whisky' in Scotland (I always struggle to remember the right version, with or without the 'e'). It is more obvious once you realise that the correct pronunciation is 'Ish-ka Baa-ha'.

As far back as medieval Ireland, early Christian monks refined basic distillation techniques, mainly to treat ailments such as colic and for relief from physical infirmities.

Over the centuries, Irish distilling evolved from small operations in monasteries to fully licensed production, with King James I granting the country's first licence in 1608.

3. TULLY'S BAR

Opened relatively recently, in 1989, this is one of the most popular bars in the city. When I filmed the pub for our socials the skies opened as if to underline the joke that Irish weather often cycles through four seasons in one day.

The temporary downpour left us completely soaked, and having to sit, sodden, and enjoy our pints in the pub's tiny snug, jokingly labelled 'Human Resources'.

Another cosy snug, a staple of almost every Irish pub.

4. THOMAS MAHER

First opened as the John Britton in 1886, before being taken over soon after by the Maher family, with Tom Maher himself becoming publican in 1929. It was a position he held until his death in December 2003 at the age of ninety-two, his seventy-seven-year tenure making him one of Ireland's longest-serving publicans.

The pub is well known for making its own whiskey, including a pre-made whiskey mac.

It was one of the last pubs in Ireland to operate a men-only counter, until the rule was lifted in 2010, leaving it with a rather curious gent's toilet door that was clearly added as an afterthought when it needed to create a second loo for the ladies.

Talking of loos, a sudden downpour caught me out early on this crawl and I had to dry my trousers under a hand dryer.

C. WATERFORD GALLERY OF ART

Housed within what was originally a bank, which opened in 1845, before later playing host to the city's first art school from 1852.

In 1939 a group of locals founded the Municipal Art Collection and, over the decades, this grew to nearly seven hundred works, showcasing everything from early twentieth-century painters, such as Jack B. Yeats and Louis le Brocquy, to contemporary Irish artists, with the pieces often moving to temporary venues across the city.

Over time, the building slowly deteriorated and, in 2019, a group of local workers transformed it into its current use as a permanent home for the collection.

5. J. & K. WALSH VICTORIAN SPIRIT GROCER

Largely unchanged since it was established in 1899, it has operated as a bar and general store, offering groceries, liquor, sweets, tobacco and local produce.

Many of the original fixtures and fittings remain, making it a spectacular tribute to yesteryear.

During the early twentieth century it was linked with nationalist activity, with then owner John Walsh hosting meetings for revolutionaries involved in the War of Independence.

D. WATERFORD

Founded by Vikings in 914 CE as a sheltered fjord haven, what was once a pivotal Norse settlement and trading port now thrives as Ireland's oldest city.

It was captured in the late twelfth century by the Normans, with Henry II making it one of Ireland's first royal cities.

With its formidable walls and stoic resistance to pretenders to the English throne, Lambert Simnel and Perkin Warbeck, between 1487 and 1495, Waterford earned the moniker 'the untaken city'.

It continued to thrive in subsequent centuries, with developments to navigate the River Suir, followed by the first glass factory in 1783, later ushering in a more industrial era.

Over the years it has survived famine, an economic shift following industrial decline, and conflicts and sieges during the Nine Years' War and the Confederate and Civil Wars.

E. CATHEDRAL OF THE MOST HOLY TRINITY WITHIN

With origins that stretch back to 1190, it is one of Ireland's oldest continuously used places of worship, and is built on the site of an earlier sixth-century church.

The decorative tower was completed in 1750, before the nineteenth century saw significant renovations of the roof, stained-glass windows and ancient walls.

It is notable as the site where Charles II was proclaimed King of Great Britain, France and Ireland following his father's execution towards the conclusion of the English Civil War.

6. THE GINGERMAN

Originally a merchant's, with origins back to the early nineteenth century, it was frequented by sailors and workers by the late 1800s, who would meet and trade over pints.

As it evolved into a public house, its ownership changed several times, and it was known as much for food as beer, until the 1960s ushered in a change when it began hosting regular trad music sessions.

The wooden beams that can be seen today were revealed and restored as part of its last significant renovation in the 1990s.

F. BEACH TOWER

Dating from the fifteenth century, this medieval tower, on a rocky outcrop, would have formed an integral part of the city's defensive walls and provided a strategic vantage point from which to monitor invading forces or pirates on the river.

It was soon adapted to facilitate its changing military use, but fell into disrepair over hundreds of years as political and naval tensions eased and the need for the defensive walls declined.

The tower was carefully restored in the 1990s following a local campaign, with the internal structure being reinforced to make it accessible.

G. CHURCH OF THE MOST HOLY TRINITY, BALLYBRICKEN

Built to replace an older, thatched chapel in 1810, before the Catholic emancipation, its 'barn-like' style was common at the time.

Its grounds were the site of both the Ballybricken Green Fair and a cattle market until 1977.

Today, the church is often referred to as the Holy Trinity 'Without' due to its position outside the medieval city walls.

7. THE HUB

Overlooking the historic Apple Market, which would have been the major trading area during medieval times, the pub is sheltered by a steel and glass canopy that was installed between 2014 and 2020 as part of a regeneration project.

The pub has won several 'best of' accolades and upstairs is a surprisingly large seating area overlooking the market.

8. GEOFF'S CAFÉ BAR

Located near the Apple Market, it was first opened as a grocer and spirit counter in 1907 by Willie Power.

Taken over in 1957 by his son Michael and daughter-in-law Eleanor, it was not until their own son, Geoff, took ownership in 1977 that it was transformed into the bar it is today.

Filled with mismatched furniture, vintage signage and artwork, it also includes a turntable behind the bar.

9. DAVY MACS

Housed within a stone cottage just off the bustling Apple Market, it emerged in its current form after a creative makeover in the early 1990s, when it was transformed from a traditional pub into the city's first dedicated gin bar.

As with most things involving gin, the exact idea and origin is unclear.

H. WATERFORD TREASURES

Located at the heart of Waterford's Viking Triangle, which is Ireland's first dedicated museum quarter, this group of sites is known collectively as the Treasures and covers over 1,100 years of the city's cultural history.

The sites that make up the Treasures are: Reginald's Tower, covered a little later in this section; virtual reality experience, the King of the Vikings; the Bishop's Palace, built in 1741, which showcases silver, glass and fine furnishings spanning hundreds of years; and four museums – the Medieval Museum, Irish Silver Museum, Irish Museum of Time and Irish Wake Museum – with collections spanning hundreds of years.

I. HOUSE OF WATERFORD

The House of Waterford is sited within a building that was first constructed as a bank in the mid-nineteenth century, before its conversion into the city's School of Art.

What had been Waterford's world-renowned glassworks industry from 1783 was revived in 1947 when skilled Europeans joined local craftsmen to re-establish the city's crystal glass heritage.

Today, the building showcases the world's largest display of Waterford crystal, which includes chandeliers, trophies and sculptures.

J. STRONGBOW AND AOIFE SCULPTURE

Representing one of Ireland's most pivotal moments, this tribute was unveiled in 2014 to honour the 1170 marriage of Richard de Clare, known as Strongbow, and Aoife MacMurrough shortly after the Norman forces captured the city.

The union of the Norman knight with the Irish princess was solemnised within Christ Church Cathedral, symbolising the blending of power, and effectively laying the groundwork for the end of Gaelic Ireland.

K. CHRIST CHURCH CATHEDRAL, CHURCH OF IRELAND

Built between 1773 and 1779 by local architect John Roberts, it stands on a site that has housed Christian worship since around 1050, when the first church was founded there by Viking settlers. It was later used as the location for the marriage of Strongbow and Princess Aoife.

A Gothic cathedral was erected around 1210 to replace the earlier church, but by the eighteenth century it was deemed outdated, so was demolished to make way for the current elegant Georgian structure, which was completed at a cost of just over £5,300.

L. JOHN CONDON MEMORIAL

This World War I monument commemorates the tragic tale of Waterford native Private John Condon, who enlisted in the Royal Irish Regiment in 1913, claiming to be older than he was.

Having been deployed to the Western Front in late 1914 he died during a gas attack at the Second Battle of Ypres on 24 May 1915. Though long believed to have been just fourteen at the time of his death, later research suggests he may have been seventeen.

Unveiled in May 2014, the sculpture pays tribute to the more than 4,800 Waterford residents who served in the war, with more than 1,100 losing their lives in the conflict.

M. WILLIAM VINCENT WALLACE PLAZA

The city's millennium project, it was named in honour of William Vincent Wallace, who was a locally born composer and not to be confused with the Scottish revolutionary played by Mel Gibson in the film *Braveheart*.

Born in 1812, Waterford's Wallace was world renowned for his expertise on both piano and violin. He went on to compose several operas, most notably *Maritana and Lurline*. After spending time across Ireland and in the United States, he died in France in 1865 and was buried in Kensal Green Cemetery in London, his tombstone bearing his own quote: 'Music is an art that knows no locality but heaven.'

N. LUKE WADDING STATUE

One of Waterford's most illustrious sons, Franciscan friar Luke Wadding was born in the city in 1588 before going on to shape European religious life primarily through his founding of St Isidore's College in Rome, which trained Irish priests from 1625.

He also played a key role in establishing St Patrick's Day on the Catholic calendar, before it became an excuse to go out to the pub.

10. JORDAN'S BAR

One of the city's oldest pubs, its licence was first issued more than three hundred years ago, although it spent much of its early life as a boarding house for workers, then known as the Parade Hotel.

After it was taken over in 1948 it acquired the nickname 'the American bar' in acknowledgement of the huge number of emigrants who would come there to book their boat tickets to the new land.

Some say it is haunted.

O. REGINALD'S TOWER

Officially the oldest civic building in Ireland, the imposing tower was built in the thirteenth century on the site of Viking foundations, both as a watch point and a symbol of the city's authority and strength.

With walls more than 10 feet thick in places, it was integrated into the city's defensive walls. However, it also served as the royal mint during medieval times, and hosted King Richard II during his visit to Ireland in 1394.

It has repelled several sieges, with a cannonball still embedded in its stonework from the Cromwellian siege of Waterford in 1650.

During the eighteenth and nineteenth centuries, it was repurposed as a prison and military storehouse, and later served as the residence of the city's constable.

Among the Viking history was a chance to step into their ancient shoes.

P. THOMAS FRANCIS MEAGHER STATUE

Erected in 2004 to commemorate the Irish nationalist leader of the Young Irelanders in the rebellion of 1848.

Following capture, he was sentenced to death, before the verdict was overturned and amended to transportation for life to Tasmania.

Escaping in 1852, he fled to the United States, where he rose through the ranks of the military, recruiting Irish migrants in his role as Brigadier General.

After the American Civil War, he was elected as a territorial governor before supposedly falling to his death from a steamboat in the Missouri River. The fact that his body was never recovered has fuelled rumours and theories that he was actually murdered by political opponents in Montana.

11. KATTY BARRY'S

Named after Kathleen 'Katty' Barry, a beloved local fishmonger with a colourful presence, who graced the quayside from the 1940s until her death in 1982.

The pub is housed in a nineteenth-century building that originally served as both a grocery and spirit store, before adopting its current name in 1973.

Q. RIVER JOHN

Also known locally as St John's River or John's Pill, the river weaves quietly through Waterford before merging with the River Suir at Adelphi Quay.

Rising in marshy lands south of the city, it travels just under four miles through a mix of suburban and hidden channels, often unnoticed beneath roads and retail parks, until it becomes visible again near Hardy's Bridge.

For centuries this slow-moving tidal stream, carved out of the shallow wetlands that once surrounded Waterford, provided access for small boats and coal barges as its gentle current meant easy passage at high tide before being carried back out.

The river declined in the mid-twentieth century, industrial waste and pollution leaving it neglected and hidden, with much of its route becoming culverted.

In recent years a community-led clean-up has breathed new life into its waters, and it now flows serenely through parks and quiet quays.

12. THE THREE SHIPPES

This pub gets its name from the three ships that once adorned Waterford's coat of arms, the symbol of a historic naval victory in the sixteenth century, when the city's forces seized three enemy galleys.

The ships also represent Waterford's importance as a naval hub for both Vikings and Normans.

The fancy Granville hotel was a perfect place to stop in the city.

DINGLE
(Marina to Dick Mack's)

One of Ireland's most picturesque towns, there is a pub almost every fifty yards and it was hard to compile a route when there was so much choice.

Starting with a view over the marina, the crawl runs in a loop through the heart of this tiny town with its pretty streets and colourful buildings.

Widely acclaimed as the best square mile of pubs in the world it is hard to disagree, as every one of these would make a top ten list in almost every place I have ever been.

On my last visit the players of the All-Ireland championship-winning Gaelic football team were celebrating here, bringing a carnival atmosphere and turning it into a town that did not sleep for days.

There are few pubs in the world as interesting as Foxy John's or Dick Mack's, which include old-fashioned shops, or Bob Griffin's, which feels like stepping back in time and into an old house.

Start at Dingle Oceanworld Aquarium (The Wood, V92 Y193).

1. **Marina Inn** *1.00 p.m.*
Strand Street, V92 EE70

2. **Bob Griffin's Bar** *1.30 p.m.*
Strand Street, V92 A091

3. **Paddy Bawn Brosnan's** *2.15 p.m.*
Strand Street, V92 E628

4. **O'Flaherty's Bar** *3.00 p.m.*
Bridge Street, V92 VK50

5. **O'Sullivan's Courthouse** *3.30 p.m.*
The Mall, V92 N471

6. **Muiris Dan's Bar** *4.15 p.m.*
14 John Street, V92 HD54

7. **An Droichead Beag** *5.00 p.m.*
Spa Road, V92 DK2E

8. **Foxy John's** *5.45 p.m.*
Main Street, V92 PD6F

9. **Curran's** *6.30 p.m.*
4 Main Street, V92 RC97

10. **Kennedy's Bar** *7.00 p.m.*
Upper Main Street, V92 P6PP

11. **McCarthys** *7.45 p.m.*
Upper Main Street, V92 YX30

12. **Dick Mack's** *8.30 p.m.*
47 Green Street, V92 FF25

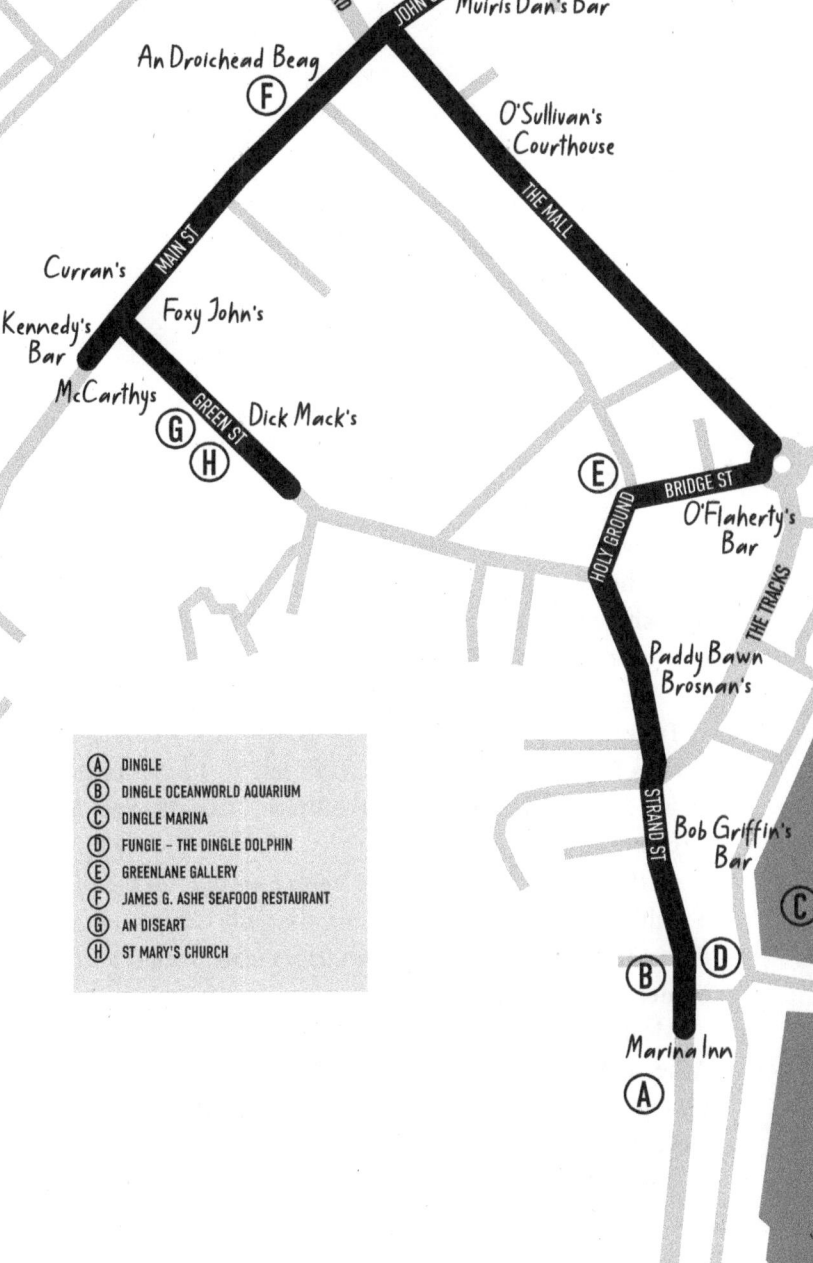

DIRECTIONS

Start overlooking the marina **(A, B, C)**, with **Marina Inn (1)** at the heart of it. Turn left out of the pub, past Fungie **(D)** opposite, and head up Strand Street with **Bob Griffin's Bar (2)** on the left opposite **Paddy Bawn Brosnan's (3)** a few doors up.

Follow the road right, past the gallery **(E)**, where **O'Flaherty's Bar (4)** is on the right. Turn left at the roundabout, where further up the blue of **O'Sullivan's Courthouse (5)** is impossible to miss.

At the end of the road, **Muiris Dan's Bar (6)** is tucked down a right-hand turning. On leaving the pub, double back to the main road and the yellow **An Droichead Beag (7)** on the corner by the stream.

Most of the remaining pubs are up the hill past James G. Ashe Seafood Restaurant **(F)**, with **Foxy John's (8)**, **Curran's (9)** and, opposite, **Kennedy's Bar (10)** a few doors down, and **McCarthys (11)** over the road.

Turn right out of the pub and head all the way down the

hill, past An Diseart **(G)**, where **Dick Mack's (12)** and the church **(H)** are opposite each other.

A. DINGLE

One of Ireland's most picturesque small towns, it is believed that the area has been inhabited since as long ago as the Bronze Age – stones, ring forts and artefacts are scattered throughout the peninsula.

The town began to take shape around the thirteenth century as the Norman conquerors began to develop it into a trading port.

Fast-forward three hundred years and it was so significant for traders from the Iberian Peninsula that it hosted their royalty ahead of the Treaty of Dingle in 1529 with King John III of Portugal.

Although Dingle continued to thrive as a centre for fishing and farming, the Great Famine of the 1840s saw the population decline either through death or emigration to the United States.

These days most visitors are from the US, often tracing their family heritage, enjoying the scenic coastal region, or taking in the locations made famous in films such as *Star Wars* and *Ryan's Daughter*.

B. DINGLE OCEANWORLD AQUARIUM

Opened in 1996, it has since expanded from its humble beginnings to become Ireland's largest public aquarium, as a team led by marine biologist Dr Kevin Flannery has overseen the introduction of sharks, penguins, piranhas, seahorses and tropical fish.

It also serves as a rehabilitation centre for sea turtles found stranded along the coastline.

C. DINGLE MARINA

The tiny town's natural harbour is well sheltered, offering safe anchorage to the population, traders and fishermen for centuries.

Although often trading overseas, or offering safe docking for Spanish and Portuguese wine and cargo ships, the fishing industry exploded throughout the nineteenth and twentieth centuries, as herring and mackerel were exported across the country, leading to the establishment of the current marina.

The start of the Wild Atlantic Way is breathtaking whatever the weather.

1. MARINA INN

Located at the head of the town's bustling pier, it was originally built in the nineteenth century, when it would have served as lodgings for local fishermen.

It was not until the mid-1990s that the building evolved into a full-time pub under the care of the Kavanagh family, who still run it today.

On a sunny day, sitting outside provides a fantastic view of the marina and the rolling green hills opposite it.

D. FUNGIE – THE DINGLE DOLPHIN

A regular visitor to the area, this solitary bottlenose dolphin became an iconic figure from the moment he was spotted in the harbour in 1983.

Although dolphins typically travel in pods, Fungie demonstrated an extraordinary bond with the locals, displaying friendliness to humans by swimming alongside their boats or interacting with swimmers.

For nearly four decades he entertained locals, remaining near the marina, leading to him being recognised as one of the longest-living solitary dolphins in the world.

A statue recognising his importance was created by American sculptor James 'Bud' Bottoms and erected in January 2000.

Sadly, Fungie disappeared without trace in 2020, although the locals still talk about him fondly.

2. BOB GRIFFIN'S BAR

Opened in 1937, the rear of the pub was also used to dry fishing nets, to prevent them from rotting.

The pub closed for a short time following the retirement of the eponymous Bob, before it was restored and reopened in 2019.

Upstairs often hosts whiskey-tasting sessions, although there is barely a level surface up the rickety stairs.

Once a family home, it is easy to imagine how it would have looked when the stove was on and an Irish stew was bubbling away.

3. PADDY BAWN BROSNAN'S

Getting its name from the legendary Gaelic footballer from Dingle, who captained Kerry to several All-Ireland victories in the 1940s, it is run by the sports star's relatives, Brian and Conor.

The front of the pub is adorned in the colours of the local team, with a mural in the beer garden paying homage to the owners' grandfather.

E. GREENLANE GALLERY

Opened by local art enthusiast Susan Callery in 1992, the gallery celebrates local artists and work inspired by the striking landscapes of West Kerry, showcased in both solo and group exhibitions.

4. O'FLAHERTY'S BAR

Opened in 1957, although the building dates to the 1860s, with the current version growing throughout the 1960s as part of the lively local music scene.

As well as being the location for many an impromptu trad band performance, it has retained its original Valentia flagstone floors.

On my last visit, the pub was serving as the meeting point for members of the marching band ahead of the town's parade to celebrate Kerry winning the All-Ireland Gaelic football trophy.

Three of the players had already starting drinking when I popped in, several hours before the start of the celebrations.

5. O'SULLIVAN'S COURTHOUSE

Another new pub in the area, having opened only in 2011 when Tommy and Saundra O'Sullivan relocated from Houston in the US.

Although serving traditional Irish fare, they have also included a Texas BBQ on the menu.

The bar features a distinctive mural on the outside, but it is inside where the *very* low ceiling showcases the scribbles of previous visitors.

Can you spot where I made my mark?

6. MUIRIS DAN'S BAR

Originally opened in the 1950s by Muiris Dan before being taken over by Tommy Griffin and Padraic Corcoran in 2004, it began as a combined pub, grocery, butcher's shop and general hardware store, with the original layout remaining today.

It was one of the top recommendations of Guinness aficionado Jason Hackett – better known by his social media persona PrimeMutton.

As wonderful as the team here were to put me and Luke up for the night when we visited to film, it was also where the winning football team stayed, so we were kept up all night by the celebrations!

7. AN DROICHEAD BEAG

With a name that translates to 'the little bridge', this is one of Dingle's most iconic pubs despite having been established in only 1986.

Like several of the town's pubs, the original building has served many roles, from a sweet shop to a butcher's – at one point it was even a milking parlour – which is reflected in the design of the beer garden, with its tiny town centre layout.

It is somewhat jokingly named 'Dingle's nightclub', as its late licence means it is the last stop for most after a day's drinking in the local pubs.

F. JAMES G. ASHE SEAFOOD RESTAURANT

Starting as a fabric store in 1849, it unusually held a liquor licence and evolved into a pub before expanding its seafood offering from 1929 under the ownership of James G. Ashe.

These days it is run by the sixth generation of the family and is filled with memorabilia, including a photo of Hollywood actor Gregory Peck, who once dined here.

8. FOXY JOHN'S

The date of its foundation is unknown, although assumed to be sometime around the late nineteenth century when it was a hardware store and bike repair centre.

Over time its use as a pub took over and its name comes from one of its longest-serving proprietors, who worked both the bar and the shop front.

Despite its antique appearance, it claims to still sell products from the hardware store, and it is one of the most unique pubs I've visited on my travels.

Keeping up the tradition of stores within pubs, there is nothing quite like Foxy John's.

9. CURRAN'S

One of the oldest pubs in the town, it was opened in 1871 as a general store and pub, with the interior having remained virtually unchanged since the 1940s.

I met a group of Americans who follow my social media, and we propped up the counter to compare ideas for Boston and Chicago pubs ahead of my travels there.

Grabbing a pint of plain on the old store counter which has now become a cosy snug.

10. KENNEDY'S BAR

Established in the 1930s by the Murphy and Kennedy families on their return from the United States, like many others it opened as a combined pub and grocery store, before it was converted into a family home.

It was not until 2014 that Michael Murphy, grandson of the original owners, decided to restore the premises and re-license it.

Rumour has it that one day there was a power cut and

since then the pub has been lit only by candlelight. A sight that might feel creepy is to be found in the garden at the rear: an abandoned building that looks like something straight out of a horror movie.

11. MCCARTHYS

With John McCarthy purchasing the premises in 1867, it stakes its claim as the oldest continuously operating pub in Dingle. However, it did briefly close for a couple of years from 2015, until it was renovated and relaunched as a regular live music venue.

I bumped into a bunch of lads from Foxy John's, who although they were on a day off, did not manage to make it very far from their local.

Plenty of stouts are available, especially this far south.

G. AN DISEART

This former convent building was converted into the Diseart Institute of Irish Spirituality and Culture in 1996, and has served as a hub for the local community.

The building was first constructed around 1886 following the arrival of the Presentation Sisters – an order of nuns founded in Cork in 1775. The chapel forms the focal point of the building and, in 1924, six stained-glass windows by artist Henry Clarke were added to depict the life of the sisters' founder Nano Nagle.

12. DICK MACK'S

Opened as a pub in 1899 by the stationmaster of the local light railway, Tom MacDonnell, it also served as a tannery, which has endured ever since, so it is no surprise that often, propped against the counter opposite the bar, is a cluster of American tourists receiving personalised belts as souvenirs.

When Tom's son Richard took over the pub, it received its famous moniker from his nickname – with the extra 'k' added for aesthetic flair.

That flair extends to the outside, where a 'walk of fame' has been created to commemorate the many stars and filmmakers who have visited, especially those from the *Ryan's Daughter* shoot in the late 1960s.

It has its own brewery to the rear, which supplies local pubs.

You know a pub is famous when it's used for directions to the church.

H. ST MARY'S CHURCH

Located at the heart of the town, this nineteenth-century neo-Gothic building was built between 1862 and 1865 by J.J. McCarthy – who designed more than eighty churches and religious buildings across Ireland.

Its foundation stone was laid on St Patrick's Day 1862, and a plaque inside commemorates Father Michael Devine, who succumbed to cholera in 1849 having courageously tended to locals afflicted by the waterborne disease.

The church underwent one of the most dramatic architectural overhauls in Ireland in 1963, as the arcades were removed and walls and elevations eliminated, ahead of structural changes in the 1970s.

BELFAST
(City Hall to the Cellars)

One of the most surprising cities I have visited on my travels, as Belfast blends a modern, vibrant atmosphere with old-world ornate architecture and a storied past.

This routes loops through the major tourist districts and includes one of the most beautiful pubs I have visited (the Crown) along with one of the most memorable (Bittles Bar).

Understandably, much of the area still has links to the decades of the Troubles and, while a reminder of sadder times, it is a brilliant and welcoming city that has become a popular tourist destination.

This Londoner found the local accent quite a challenge, but there were plenty of laughs to be had.

When we finished filming the route for our social media, it was back into the heart of the Cathedral Quarter to dance the night away at the Dirty Onion before tumbling into the Foundry Hotel, which is on the site of the original Harp brewery opposite.

Start at the Europa Hotel (BT2 7AP).

1. **The Crown Liquor Saloon** *1.00 p.m.*
46 Great Victoria Street, BT2 7BA

2. **The Garrick** *1.45 p.m.*
29 Chichester Street, BT1 4JB

3. **Bittles Bar** *2.15 p.m.*
70 Upper Church Lane, BT1 4QL

4. **The Morning Star** *3.00 p.m.*
17–19 Pottinger's Entry, BT1 4DT

5. **Whites Tavern** *3.30 p.m.*
2–4 Winecellar Entry, BT1 1QN

6. **The Dirty Onion** *4.15 p.m.*
3 Hill Street, BT1 2LA

7. **Harp Bar (closed Mon)** *5.00 p.m.*
35 Hill Street, BT1 2NB

8. **Duke of York** *5.30 p.m.*
7–11 Commercial Court, BT1 2NB

9. **The John Hewitt (closed Mon)** *6.00 p.m.*
51 Donegall Street, BT1 2FH

10. **Sunflower** *6.30 p.m.*
65 Union Street, BT1 2JG

11. **Kelly's Cellars** *7.15 p.m.*
30–32 Bank Street, BT1 1HL

12. **Madden's Bar** *8.00 p.m.*
74 Berry Street, BT1 1FJ

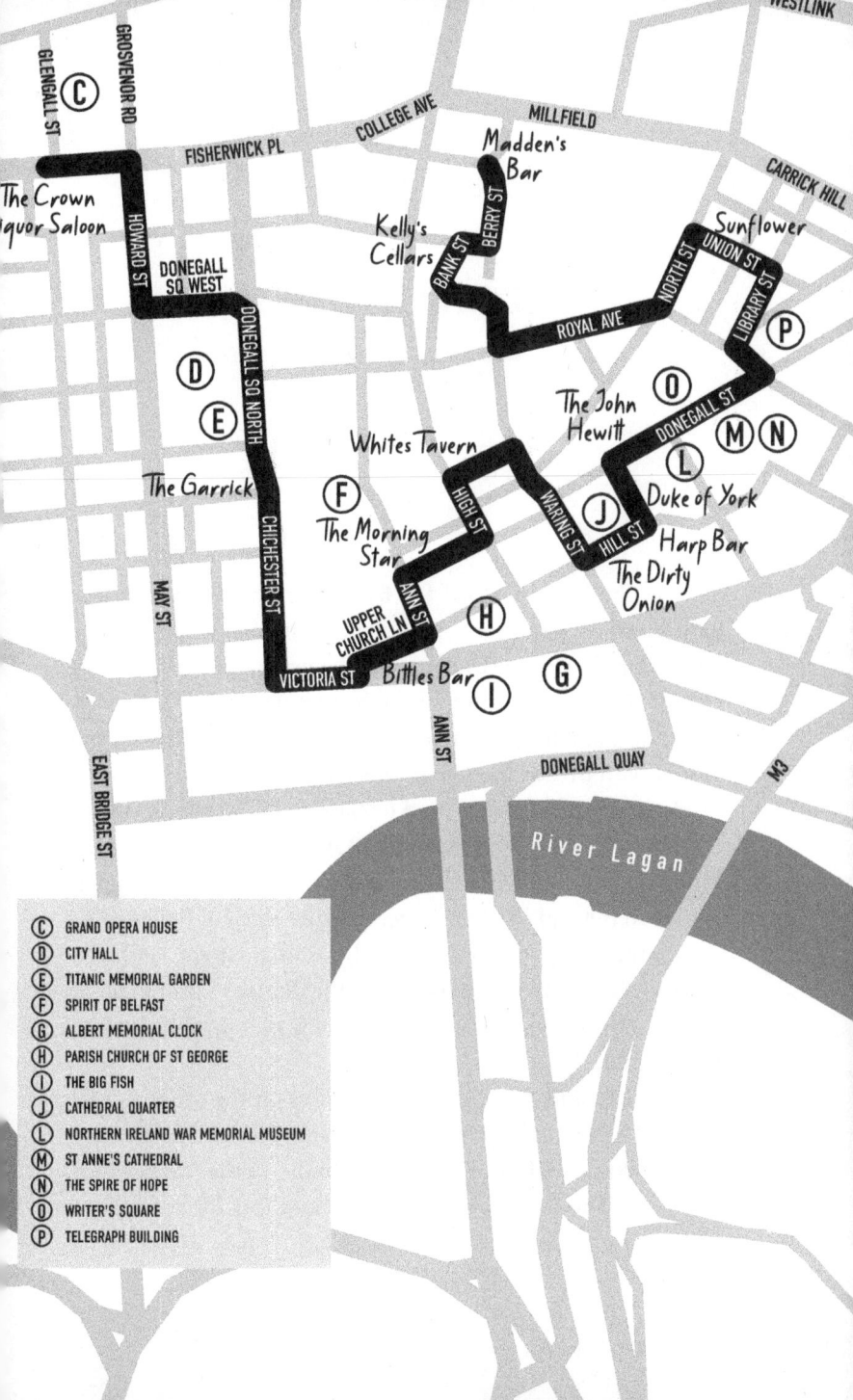

DIRECTIONS

Start at the Europa Hotel **(A, B)**, where **The Crown Liquor Saloon (1)** is opposite. Turn right from the pub, past the Grand Opera House **(C)**, and take the first right towards City Hall **(D, E)**. After heading across the grounds to the far corner, continue along the main road, where **The Garrick (2)** is on the corner with **Bittles Bar (3)** on the left at the end of the road.

Head along the small road to the left of the pub and take the first left where **The Morning Star (4)** is down Pottinger's Entry on the right. Before turning down this alley, a quick detour to the end of the road reaches the *Spirit of Belfast* **(F)**.

Continue past the pub to reach the high street, with the Albert Memorial Clock **(G)** and the Parish Church of St George (**H**) to the right and, for a quick detour, the *Big Fish* **(I)** behind it.

Turn left, and along Winecellar Entry on the other side of the road is **Whites Tavern (5)**. Turn right at the end of the alley before taking a left up Hill Street into the Cathedral Quarter **(J)**, where **The Dirty Onion (6)** and **Harp Bar (7)** are next to each other, with the **Duke of York (8, K)** along the first left.

Turn right at the end of the road to reach **The John Hewitt (9)** just before the Northern Ireland War Memorial Museum **(L)** to the side of the cathedral **(M, N)** opposite Writer's Square **(O)**. Continue along the road and follow it left, before turning right up Library Street and past the Telegraph Building **(P)**, where the **Sunflower (10)** is on the corner of the first left.

Past the pub, turn left at North Street, before turning right at the traffic lights down Royal Avenue. At the first crossroads turn right into a mainly pedestrian area, along which are **Kelly's Cellars (11)** and **Madden's Bar (12)**.

A. BELFAST

The capital city of Northern Ireland, it is a historically significant port, with shipbuilders Harland & Wolff responsible for RMS *Titanic*.

The shipyard's humongous gantry cranes, named after biblical figures Samson and Goliath, are impossible to miss on flights heading into City Airport, as they stand a whopping 348 and 315 feet tall, respectively.

Belfast is politically and culturally significant having been central to the Troubles – a period of conflict that shaped much of the modern history. The peace walls that separated the sectarian divisions still stand as a reminder of the times.

The city is full of beautiful historic buildings such as the City Hall, Queen's University and the Grand Opera House, alongside street art and murals.

I adored the vibrant buzz in the city, although found the accent much harder to understand than the Dublin accent I am more accustomed to.

Probably the most famous ship of all time; I had the opportunity for my Titanic *moment while filming here.*

B. GEORGE BEST BELFAST CITY AIRPORT

It is just a short taxi ride into the city from here, which probably makes it the only occasion I have flown on a budget airline and landed in the vicinity of a destination and not a two-hour coach journey away.

It is named after the legendary footballer George Best, who was born in the city, with the former Manchester United player widely regarded as one of the greatest of all time.

Although his career and later life were marred by his playboy image, it did produce some memorable quotes, such as 'In 1969 I gave up women and alcohol – it was the worst 20 minutes of my life' and 'I spent a lot of money on booze, birds and fast cars. The rest I just squandered.'

1. THE CROWN LIQUOR SALOON

One of the most famous pubs in Belfast, this Victorian-era gem dates to the 1820s.

It was originally called the Railway Tavern, but when it was renovated by its new owners in 1885, legend claims that its new name was immortalised in the floor mosaic at the entrance so that patrons would tread their muddy feet on the crown in a humorous insult to British royalty.

The pub is famous for its lavish décor, with ornate stained-glass windows, intricately carved woodwork, old-fashioned gas lamps and marble-tiled floors. The layout of the pub features ten cosy snugs that would have been built to accommodate the pub's more reserved customers during the austere Victorian period. Under the bar, hot water was pumped through a long metal pipe on which workers would dry their feet.

Although run by a pub company, it is now owned by the National Trust.

C. GRAND OPERA HOUSE

Opened in 1895, it was designed by renowned theatre architect Frank Matcham, who was responsible for ninety theatres across the UK – far more than any other architect at the time.

It is most famous for its ornate interior, which blends several styles, such as Baroque, Flemish and Indian, alongside intricate plasterwork.

This spectacular venue has hosted the likes of Charlie Chaplin, Laurel and Hardy, and Dame Judi Dench. It was also the location of Luciano Pavarotti's professional UK debut.

D. CITY HALL

Built on the site of the old linen exchange in 1906, it was constructed to reflect Belfast's new city status granted by Queen Victoria in 1888.

The building is a stunning example of Baroque Revival architecture, with a grand dome that rises to 173 feet, and intricate stonework, all sited within landscaped gardens that make it a notable destination for tourists.

Although it does offer free public access for those who wish to enter and admire the stained-glass windows, we don't have time for that – we've got pubs to go to.

E. *TITANIC* MEMORIAL GARDEN

Officially opened in 2012 to mark the centenary of the sinking of the RMS *Titanic*, it incorporates a 1920 memorial statue, and includes a plinth bearing fifteen bronze plaques inscribed with the names of all 1,512 people who perished. It is the only memorial in the world to list every victim of the disaster, regardless of their class or nationality.

2. THE GARRICK

One of the city's oldest pubs, it was established in 1870, having been the site of a builder's merchants that specialised in marble and stone.

It is hard to believe this previous life, as the pub now extends into a large dining room to the rear, and the bar area is ornately decorated with dark wood panelling and Venetian mirrors.

On my visit, the pub served both an Irish coffee and a Belfast coffee, the latter containing cold brew (rather than hot) and poitín (instead of whiskey). Both, of course, topped with thick double cream.

3. BITTLES BAR

One of the city's most famous bars, it was established in 1868 and is instantly recognisable as a mini-version of New York's Flatiron Building. Prior to that, it had operated as a warehouse for a flour merchant.

It was originally opened as a gin palace called the Shakespeare, largely due to its theatre-going clientele, but more recently has become filled with knick-knacks and memorabilia under the stewardship of John Bittles, who took it over aged twenty-nine in the 1990s.

The landlord is notorious for previously not serving cola or half pints, with one local I met having received the latter only because of a doctor's note.

At the height of the Troubles in 1973, the pub was targeted when a Molotov cocktail was thrown through the letterbox. The perpetrator, Alan Lundy, was convicted of the attack and later killed in an unrelated shooting.

This was the pub I was most nervous about visiting, as John is widely known for his 'candid' demeanour and has become something of a local legend. But he could not have been more welcoming as I sat with him and shared a pint in this tiny pub, which holds barely more than twenty people.

4. THE MORNING STAR

Established in 1810 as a coaching inn, it is hard to believe such a large pub can hide down such a tiny alleyway – known as Pottinger's Entry.

It would have served the Belfast-to-Dublin mail coach, and its name is said to come from the sight of sunrise as the postal workers reached the city, before stopping here to rest.

It was taken over in 1989 by the McAlister family, who are sixth-generation farmers, leading to the pub offering a comparatively wide range of locally sourced food – there was a delicious-smelling carvery on offer when I visited, but it was far too early to stop for food!

The iconic Guinness is part of the essence of Ireland.

F. *SPIRIT OF BELFAST*

Unveiled in 2009, the sculpture was created by New York artist Dan George and is often referred to locally as 'the onion rings' due to its looping, interwoven steel design.

G. ALBERT MEMORIAL CLOCK

Quick Irish wit has given this memorial tower, which was built in 1869 in memory of Queen Victoria's consort, the nickname 'Belfast's leaning tower' as, over the years, the shifting of the reclaimed land it stands on has given it a slight tilt. Although, at four pints into the crawl, it is hard to see the lean.

H. PARISH CHURCH OF ST GEORGE

Belfast's oldest Anglican church because, although this version was built in 1816, there has been a chapel here since at least 1306. The various iterations of the church saw King William of Orange attend a service in 1690 on his route to the Battle of the Boyne.

The current building has survived the Belfast Blitz during World War II and the detonation of a 150 lb bomb during the Troubles.

I. THE *BIG FISH*

Also known as the *Salmon of Knowledge*, this popular public artwork was created by John Kindness in 1999 and sits on Donegall Quay overlooking the River Lagan. One of the main rivers of Northern Ireland, the Lagan was an important waterway in terms of supporting the area's major shipbuilding industry.

The scales of the 33-foot-long mosaic depict scenes from the city's history, local stories and imprints of newspaper clippings.

5. WHITES TAVERN

Claiming to be the oldest tavern in Belfast and, although its licence dates to 1630, the current structure is believed to be from around 1790 when it was used as a wine store, before becoming an oyster room.

It has connections to Irish revolutionaries and is said to be the place where leader of the United Irishmen Movement, Henry Joy McCracken, stopped for a final drink on the way to his execution in 1798.

It is hidden down one of the city's narrow alleyways, which were typically called 'entries' and serviced the dense residential and commercial development when Belfast was first laid out.

The pub has been featured in several TV shows and films, and hosted Bill and Hillary Clinton when they visited in 2023 to celebrate the twenty-fifth anniversary of the Good Friday Agreement.

Following extensive renovation from 2020, the venue now includes a garden under a retractable roof, a beer hall and Ireland's first Guinness-only bar.

J. CATHEDRAL QUARTER

Originally the hub of trade for the linen and shipbuilding industries, it has been transformed into a vibrant area to celebrate the arts, with the opening of galleries, museums and performance spaces – notably hosting the Cathedral Quarter Arts Festival each year.

With pubs proudly showing off their whiskey selection, most nights deserve a nightcap.

6. THE DIRTY ONION

One of the more unique venues I have been too, this pub lives inside one of the city's oldest structures, with the building said to date to 1780.

It was originally the site of a warehouse; these days large steel and wooden beams span the beer garden to support the crumbling walls.

This was the perfect place for a stop at Yardbird upstairs, which has all sorts of rotisserie chicken and I, of course, gave its famous Spice Bag a try.

7. HARP BAR

The original Harp Bar was an important venue for the local punk rock scene during the 1970s–1980s, located in what is now the Foundry Hotel, where I stayed on my last visit to the city.

Its rich musical heritage saw it compared favourably to legendary venues like London's Roxy Club and NYC's CBGB.

The local scene began to wane, leading to the venue's closure in the 1990s, before it was reinstated in 2013, a few yards down the road, in the original Harp Lager offices.

Inside, the new version is fitted out with dark wood panelling, antique mirrors and red velvet wallpaper, making it the perfect place for date night – but that's not why we're here, we're here for beer.

8. DUKE OF YORK

Nestled halfway down one of the city's most Instagrammable streets, Commercial Court, with its street art, murals, neon lights and colourful umbrellas.

The pub is crammed full of memorabilia and Belfast artefacts, but despite its old-world charm it is in fact a rebuilt version, as the earlier two-hundred-year-old pub was destroyed in 1972 by the accidental explosion of a bomb that was intended for the High Court but detonated here prematurely.

I was lucky to grab a seat in the tiny snug, nicknamed 'the office', which is full of tributes to local band Snow Patrol, who played their first gig here in 1998 as part of a festival for local artists. To the side of the pub, there is a small plaque that was unveiled in 2010 to commemorate the gig.

On my last visit, I was lucky to have a guide who took me to the courtyard over the street, where there is a humorous mural of some of the most famous political leaders, before we popped into the whiskey store on the corner for a tasting.

The pub that gave Snow Patrol their first chance honours them in the snug.

K. SNOW PATROL

Formed in 1994, under the name Shrug and then Polar Bear, the band members met while studying at Dundee University.

They are best known for their single 'Chasing Cars', which, as of 2025, is the most played twenty-first-century song on UK radio.

9. THE JOHN HEWITT

This reasonably modern pub was established in 1999 as a social enterprise, as it was owned by the Belfast Unemployed Resource Centre.

Its name honours the late poet and socialist John Hewitt, and it has since been taken over by Belfast's first cooperative brewery, Boundary Brewing.

L. NORTHERN IRELAND WAR MEMORIAL MUSEUM

With approximately 300,000 US troops stationed in Northern Ireland between 1942 and 1945, this museum pays tribute to the area's significant contribution to World War II.

It highlights the involvement of local men and women in the armed forces and the Home Front, and the impact of the Belfast Blitz in 1941, during which hundreds of lives were lost and much of the city was damaged.

M. ST ANNE'S CATHEDRAL

Home to Northern Ireland's second-largest pipe organ – the largest being located in St Peter's Parish Church just outside the city – construction started in 1899 and it incorporated the existing parish church.

The semicircular arches and basilica layout are typical of the Romanesque design that was popular at the time. However, its foundations were unusual, with the soft clay forcing the addition of deep wooden piles.

N. THE *SPIRE OF HOPE*

The stainless-steel structure stands 131 feet tall and was installed on the roof of St Anne's Cathedral in 2007, to mark the cathedral's completion after nearly one hundred years of construction.

It was designed by Colin Conn and Robert Jamison of Box Architects, who won a competition for Irish architects under the age of forty.

O. WRITER'S SQUARE

Created in 2002 to celebrate Belfast's rich literary history, it features quotations engraved in stone from some of the region's most celebrated writers, such as C. S. Lewis, playwright Stewart Parker and novelist Brian Moore.

Given that it can hold around a thousand people it is often the location for festivals and concerts.

P. TELEGRAPH BUILDING

Built in the late nineteenth century, it served as the headquarters for the *Belfast Telegraph*, which was founded in 1870 and became one of Northern Ireland's most prominent newspapers.

10. SUNFLOWER

This pub is instantly recognisable by the original green 1980s security cage covering the entrance – a remnant of the Troubles – which would have enabled staff to monitor patrons before entry.

Despite this sad reminder, it proudly displays a sign on its outside wall reading, 'No topless bathing – Ulster has suffered enough' – a typical example of Belfast wit.

There has been a pub on the site since the late 1800s, when it was known as both the Tavern and the Avenue, before the current version was opened in 2012 and went on to win CAMRA's Pub of the Year award just a year later.

It famously doesn't serve Guinness, with legend saying this comes from a bet between owners who said that you couldn't run an Irish pub without serving pints of the popular black stuff.

I grabbed a pint of Beamish instead and sat in the lively beer garden for one of its award-winning pizzas.

11. KELLY'S CELLARS

This was one of the most requested pubs on social media before I made the trip, and when I got there I could see why.

Dating back to 1720, it was originally a bonded store for whiskey and has retained much of its original character, such as the uncomfortably low archways, whitewashed stone walls and open fireplaces.

It is steeped in revolutionary history, as it was said to be the meeting place for the Society of United Irishmen who were behind the 1798 rebellion. Legend has it that the organiser, Henry Joy McCracken, hid behind the bar to evade capture by British soldiers.

12. MADDEN'S BAR

Although there are claims of a pub on the site as far back as the 1750s, the current establishment was taken over by the Madden family in the 1870s.

A hidden gem, it is often hailed as one of the city's most cherished authentic pubs, with traditional live music and comedy nights either downstairs among the drinkers or in a large bar upstairs.

Like many visitors, I was caught out by the unique entry system, wondering why the door would not open, until some friendly smokers outside pointed out that I needed to press the buzzer to be let in.

Now a sad reminder of what it would have been like during the Troubles, this would have been essential at the time, as the pub was often at the heart of the conflict.

Over a pint, the current owner shared a few tales with me, of nearby car bombings and drive-by shootings, that are now thankfully a long time behind us.

On the side of the pub is a tribute to Art Lundy, who was a renowned fiddler from the city, and it features the phrase 'Fáilte isteach', which means 'Welcome in'.

DERRY
(Peace Bridge to the Walls)

This historic place is famous for the seventeenth-century walls that encircle the old city centre, and our route passes through them several times.

Named UK City of Culture in 2013, it has a young, vibrant arts and music scene, and many of the pubs along this route host live music and dancing.

Although officially called Londonderry, I have decided to refer to it throughout this chapter as Derry – not as a political statement, but having gathered the opinions of the people who live there and run the pubs.

Its sad history saw some of the most heated clashes of the Troubles, including the Bloody Sunday massacre. But despite this still being relatively recent history, the pubs along this route are some of the friendliest I have visited.

I especially enjoyed the final stretch along Waterloo Street, where I would place O'Loughlin's (and its Wee Bar) among my very favourite spots.

Start at Derry Station (BT47 6AH).

1. **The Corner House Pub & Lounge** *1.30 p.m.*
Ebrington Hotel, 69–72 Ebrington Square, BT47 6FA

2. **Guildhall Taphouse** *2.00 p.m.*
4 Custom House Street, BT48 6AA

3. **Tinneys Bar & The Shirt Factory** *2.30 p.m.*
4 Patrick Street, BT48 7EL

4. **The Derby Bar** *3.00 p.m.*
63 Great James Street, BT48 7DF

5. **The Rocking Chair** *4.00 p.m.*
15–17 Waterloo Street, BT48 6HA

6. **Badgers Bar** *4.45 p.m.*
18 Orchard Street, BT48 6EG

7. **Blackbird** *5.30 p.m.*
24 Foyle Street, BT48 6AL

8. **River Inn** *6.15 p.m.*
34–38 Shipquay Street, BT48 6DW

9. **O'Loughlin's (main pub open Thurs–Sun)** *7.00 p.m.*
27–31 Waterloo Street, BT48 6HA

10. **Lizzie O'Farrell's** *7.45 p.m.*
26 Waterloo Street, BT48 6HF

11. **The Dungloe Bar** *8.15 p.m.*
41–43 Waterloo Street, BT48 6HD

12. **Peadar O'Donnell's** *9.00 p.m.*
63 Waterloo Street, BT48 6HD

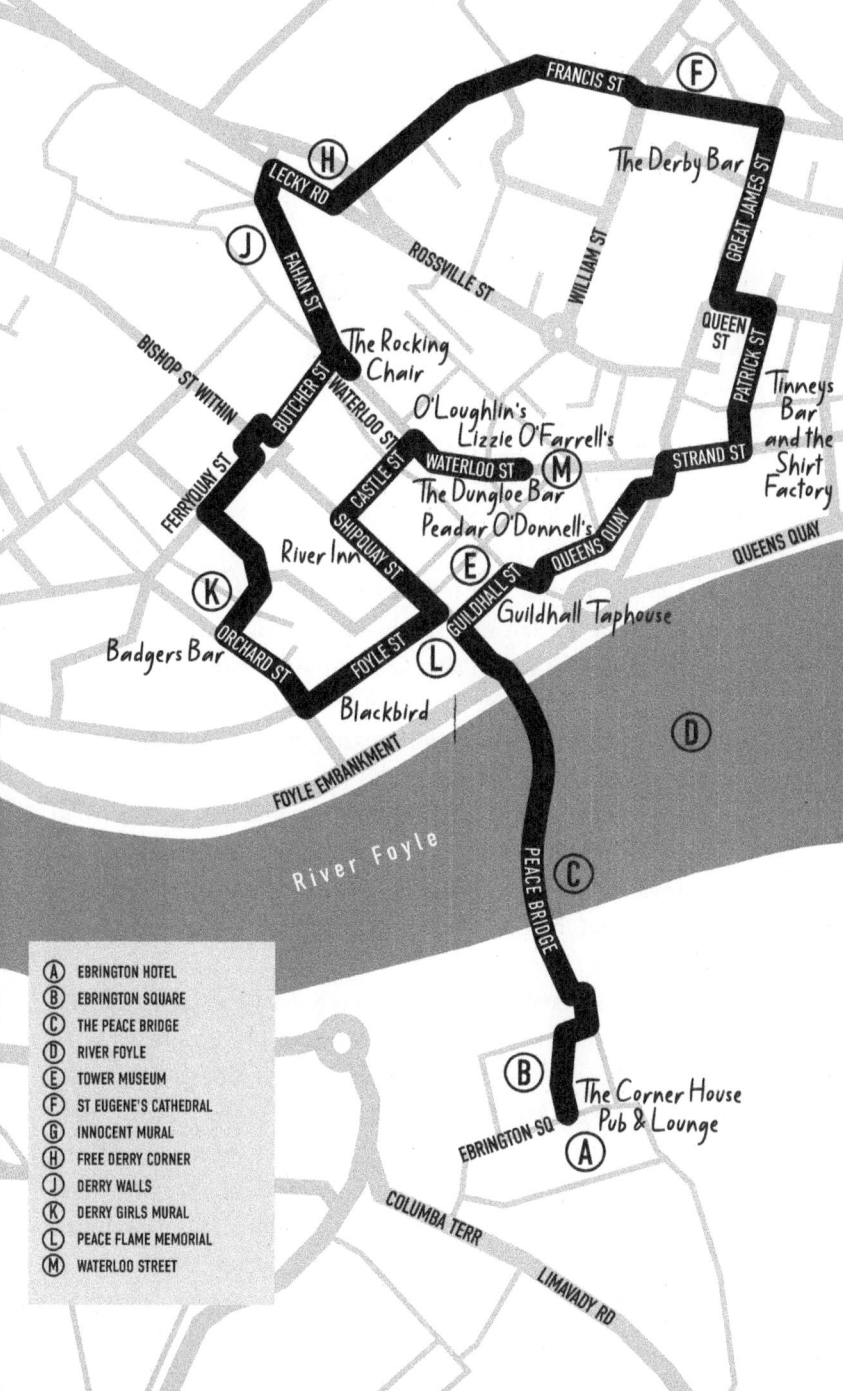

DIRECTIONS

Start at the station and walk up the hill along the path, with the river on the left and the Ebrington Hotel **(A)** at the top of the square **(B)**, with **The Cornerhouse Pub & Lounge (1)** alongside it. Head over the Peace Bridge **(C, D)**, and along the alley opposite the pedestrian crossing is **Guildhall Taphouse (2)** near the Tower Museum **(E)**.

Head through the pedestrian area and follow the road before turning left past the lights, down Patrick Street to **Tinneys Bar (3)**. Continue past the pub and turn left onto Queen Street, before turning right up the hill to **The Derby Bar (4)**.

Take the next left behind the pub, past the cathedral **(F)**, and follow the road over the roundabout to Bogside **(G, H, I)**. Cross the green and head up Fahan Street alongside the city walls **(J)**, where **The Rocking Chair (5)** is at the top of Waterloo Street.

Head back through the stone archway of the walls and, continuing straight, pass through another stone archway, before turning left at the shopping centre and down the hill to **Badgers Bar (6, K)**, with **Blackbird (7)** left at the next junction.

Continue past the pub before turning left at the Peace Flame memorial **(L)**, where **River Inn (8)** is just past the walls.

Take the first right up Castle Street before emerging at Waterloo Street **(M)**, where **O'Loughlin's (9)** is opposite **Lizzie O'Farrell's (10)**, with **The Dungloe Bar (11)** a few doors down and **Peadar O'Donnell's (12)** at the bottom of the road.

A. EBRINGTON HOTEL

A luxurious four-star hotel, it opened in 2023 as part of the regeneration of the site of the old barracks. The project cost more than £15 million and included the restoration of several nineteenth-century buildings – including the clock tower.

B. EBRINGTON SQUARE

Originally an orchard, the area was occupied by King James II's forces during the so-called Great Siege of Derry in 1689, when they strategically positioned their cannons to fire into the walled city on the other side of the river.

It became a full-time barracks in 1841 and played a crucial role in both world wars, where it operated as an anti-submarine training base until its closure in 2003 and subsequent transformation into a public space in 2011.

The square neighbours an illuminated art exhibit called *Mute Meadow*, created by internationally acclaimed artists Vong Phaophanit and Claire Oboussier. The forty pairs of angled steel columns stand between 20 and 30 feet tall and originally formed a 'forest of light', intended to symbolise the city's journey from conflict to peace. However, with the lights going out just a year after its unveiling in 2011, it has since fallen into disrepair with no plan in place to restore the artwork.

1. THE CORNERHOUSE PUB & LOUNGE

Part of the Ebrington Hotel, it was originally the home of the captain when the area was transformed into a barracks – although, when looked at square on, it was obviously quite a small house.

Although the house was built around the same time as the barracks, it was not converted into a pub until the opening of the hotel in 2023.

On our visit we managed to get up to the roof terrace, which, while being basic and unfurnished, provides a sensational view of the city.

Although a modest layout, this balcony offers one of the best views over Derry.

C. THE PEACE BRIDGE

Opened in 2011, this pedestrian and cycle bridge was constructed to connect the city centre with the redesigned square opposite.

Part of a broader regeneration project, its location symbolically joins the predominantly nationalist city side with the majority unionist Waterside. The design sees two structural arms stretching from either bank before meeting in the middle, a deliberate metaphor for the two communities coming together.

D. RIVER FOYLE

Considered one of the best salmon rivers in Europe, it stretches for about 20 miles and has historically played a crucial part in the economy as well as forming a strategic military border.

In the 1689 Siege of Derry, ships broke through the barricades to bring food and supplies to the then starving city.

2. GUILDHALL TAPHOUSE

Housed in a nineteenth-century merchant building, it was formerly called the Monico Bar and claims to be the city's first dedicated craft beer and cocktail bar.

As well as being a hub for live music, its range of craft beers includes its own signature ales and lagers brewed under the name Dopey Dick, in a playful dig at the killer whale that unfortunately lost its bearings and swam up the river in 1997 in search of salmon. Officially known as 'Comet', he was discovered 40 years later living in a pod off the West coast of Scotland.

E. TOWER MUSEUM

Dedicated to the local history of the city, the museum opened in 1992 on the site of the original O'Doherty Tower, which would have been one of the main structures in the historic fortifications.

It features a permanent exhibition, 'The Story of Derry', which traces the city's history from its settlement to recent times. Up until recently it also hosted 'An Armada Shipwreck', featuring tales and artefacts from the 1588 sinking of Spanish Armada ship *La Trinidad Valencera*, whose wreck was rediscovered in 1971. Currently closed, this exhibition is due to be relocated to the city's new Derry-Londonderry North Atlantic (DNA) Museum on Ebrington Square, which it is hoped will open in autumn 2026.

3. TINNEY'S BAR & THE SHIRT FACTORY

Established in 1847, making it the oldest family-owned pub in Derry City, it is part of a tongue-in-cheek holy trinity of pub, bookies and takeaway all side by side!

Its upstairs function room pays homage to the city's shirt factory heritage, which emerged in the nineteenth century and became a cornerstone of the city's economy and identity.

It started in 1831 when William Scott, a master weaver from Ballougry, started producing linen-fronted cotton shirts with his family.

As demand rose from large cities like Glasgow and London, he pioneered an expanded production network, hiring women to sew shirts in their own homes. It was effectively one of the first examples of the gig economy and home working, with the 'factory girls' often becoming their family's main earners.

Supported by these home workers, he expanded his main operation to larger premises that employed more than 750 people by the 1840s.

The advent of accessible sewing machines saw the industry explode, and in 1857 the largest shirt factory in the world opened on Foyle Road, housing 1,400 workers, with an additional 3,000 supporting what was now the city's main economy.

The factory girls were among the first unionised female workers in the country, and the industry peaked in the 1920s before competition during the mid-twentieth century led to the closure of the last major factory, Desmonds, in 2003.

4. THE DERBY BAR

Originally called the Errigle Inn, the pub was established in 1894, although parts of the building date back to the sixteenth century.

Throughout the interior are snugs and multiple rooms branching off from the main bar area, where the barman regaled me with tales of ghostly goings-on – despite the fact that I could not pick up a word, thanks to his strong accent.

F. ST EUGENE'S CATHEDRAL

Completed in 1873, it serves as the mother church of the Diocese of Derry. It was built in the Gothic Revival style, with the cathedral's spire dominating the city's skyline.

It is dedicated to St Eugene, the patron saint of the diocese, who was one of the pioneers of the early Irish Church. Also known as St Eógan or Eoghan, he was a sixth-century saint who founded a monastery in present-day County Tyrone.

G. *INNOCENT* MURAL

Painted on the gable wall that was briefly home to the Mike Jackson *War Criminal* mural, this latest version was unveiled in June 2023 as a poignant tribute to the fourteen civilians who lost their lives on Bloody Sunday.

Central to the mural is the image of seventeen-year-old Gerald Donaghey, part of the campaign to clear his name as his death was mired in many posthumous allegations, with soldiers claiming he had been in possession of nail bombs.

He was widely described as a quiet and engaged young man, interested in political activism, and his death was ruled as wrong and unjustifiable by the Saville Inquiry into the tragedy.

The image forms part of the famous People's Gallery, which is a series of murals reflecting Derry's turbulent past.

H. FREE DERRY CORNER

Among the iconic murals in this area stands this simple gable wall painted with the slogan: 'You are now entering Free Derry.'

It was first painted in January 1969 by activist Liam Hillen and stood as a defiant marker of the entrance to the self-declared autonomous nationalist area known as Free Derry during the early years of the Troubles.

The slogan was inspired by civil rights movements abroad, particularly the Free Speech Movement at the University of California, Berkeley, where Eamonn McCann used the phrase in 1964.

Hillen's original version was not neat, so signwriter John 'Caker' Casey professionally repainted it in block capital letters ahead of a visit by then British Home Secretary James Callaghan in 1969.

The act marked the beginning of a period known as 'Free Derry', during which the Bogside area operated as a self-declared autonomous zone from 1969 to 1972. During this time, residents erected barricades and maintained control over the area, resisting entry by British security forces. The area became a focal point for civil rights activism and was the site of significant events, including the Battle of the Bogside in 1969 and Bloody Sunday in 1972.

I. BLOODY SUNDAY

This tragic event occurred on 30 January 1972 during a civil rights march in the Bogside area to protest the 'internment without trial' policy introduced by the ruling British government.

As thousands descended on the Guildhall, tensions began to rise due to the ban on public marches, with young protestors said to have thrown stones at the army barricades.

Without warning, soldiers from the 1st Battalion, Parachute Regiment were ordered to move in and arrest rioters before opening fire with live ammunition at the unarmed civilians.

Of those in the firing line, thirteen died on the day, with a fourteenth passing away a few months later from the injuries he had sustained. All of those shot were civilians, and seven of them were teenagers.

The event deeply shocked the world, and among the intensity of the Troubles it deepened sectarian divisions and significantly boosted support for the IRA.

The initial official investigation, the Widgery Tribunal, was widely discredited as a whitewash and it was not until a twelve-year investigation by the Saville Inquiry ended in 2010, that the British government officially acknowledged that the killings were 'unjustified and unjustifiable'.

At the end of the inquiry, then Prime Minister David Cameron issued a formal apology on behalf of the British state.

It is heartbreaking to imagine such a distressing event occurring, in such recent times, in a city where this Londoner was made to feel so welcome in every pub I went to.

J. DERRY WALLS

Among the best-preserved city walls in Europe, they were built between 1613 and 1619 by English settlers during the Plantation of Ulster.

The walls stretch for about a mile, encircling the old city to protect it from attacks. Featuring seven original gatehouses, also remaining in place are cannons and historic bastions.

The most famous cannon, Roaring Meg, was cast in 1642 using funds from the Fishmongers' Company of London and was pointed towards Bogside during the 105-day blockade by the forces of King James II.

5. THE ROCKING CHAIR

Affectionately known as 'The Rocker' among locals, this pub is nestled just outside the historic city walls and overlooks the Bogside.

It was the location for early performances by punk band the Undertones, best known for their worldwide hit 'Teenage Kicks'. The song is notable as the favourite of the late Radio 1 DJ Peel, who reportedly burst into tears upon first hearing it and, on one occasion, played it twice in a row.

6. BADGERS BAR

This comparatively new pub was only established in 1979, by Hugh McDaid, who began his career as a delivery boy for Doherty's Butchers before purchasing the pub, whose name is derived from his nickname when his hair started to turn grey in his twenties.

Ironically for his two sons, who now run the pub, one has dark hair and the other is grey.

K. *DERRY GIRLS* MURAL

This humorous tribute to the hit TV series *Derry Girls*, is impossible to miss on the side of Badgers Bar.

Despite local protests at the time, the mural has remained as a homage to the show and its five main characters – Erin, Orla, Clare, Michelle and James – who appear in their school uniforms.

The critically acclaimed Northern Irish sitcom was created by Lisa McGee, with three series aired on Channel 4 between 2018 and 2022.

Set during the 1990s, the show follows the five teenagers as they navigate adolescence against the backdrop of the Troubles.

It has resonated with audiences worldwide, becoming Channel 4's most successful comedy since *Father Ted*.

7. BLACKBIRD

A new pub that was opened in the 2010s on the site of Beckett's Bar, it attained number twenty-eight on the best UK bars list according to a private poll run by Liberty Games.

There was barely any room to sit when I visited, and this lively place has an opening at the rear of the bar, with the floor lit by coloured glass, which is where I picked up my pint.

L. PEACE FLAME MEMORIAL

Unveiled in 2013 as part of Derry's year as UK City of Culture, it is one of only a few eternal flames in the world dedicated to peace.

The inauguration ceremony saw it lit by Catholic and Protestant children, in the presence of Martin Luther King III, son of the civil rights leader.

8. RIVER INN

Derry's oldest sited bar, established in 1684. At the time of its founding, there were three essential requirements for establishments to receive an 'Inn's Licence' – they needed permission to sell punch, offer accommodation and stable horses.

It predates the siege of Derry, which is depicted on a large copper plaque alongside a 1690 map of the city, etched on a mirror in the bar.

At one point, its small bar was named the Gluepot after the renowned London pub. However, the tenure of the Doherty family, who have run it for the last forty years, has seen extensive developments, including the incorporation of the adjoining Palace Cinema, to create a complex of different venues under one roof.

In 1798, the inn's cellars were notably used to detain Irish revolutionary Wolfe Tone, a leading figure in the Irish Rebellion, before he was transferred to Dublin for execution.

M. WATERLOO STREET

It is hard to believe that today's steep street used to lead out of the city walls and into marshy land where cattle grazed – giving it the name Cowbog Street.

It was renamed in honour of the famous battle of 1815, with the street being pedestrianised not long after.

Although now known for its vibrant nightlife, in the 1950s it was mostly occupied by retail premises run by the large population of Indian people who had settled in Derry at the time.

9. O'LOUGHLIN'S

This vibrant addition to the Waterloo Street nightlife is open Thursday to Sunday, although the delightful Wee Bar next door is open all week.

Although not a particularly old pub, the owners told me they are not open all week because they spend the rest of their time scouring the island for knick-knacks and memorabilia. They are obviously highly successful at it, as the walls are barely visible.

The Bogside Snug contains the original front door from the Bogside Inn, which was positioned at the heart of the Bogside and bore witness to many of the pivotal events during the Troubles, including the Battle of the Bogside in 1969 and Bloody Sunday in 1972.

The inn was demolished in 2021 as part of a regeneration project, and the owner of O'Loughlin's managed to acquire the door at a local antiques auction.

Its small beer garden has a mini version of the 'Free Derry' mural and a fantastic view across the city.

10. LIZZIE O'FARRELL'S

This lively corner pub is renowned for its live music scene, with Club Lizzie upstairs a popular spot with locals.

It was formerly known as the Castle Bar, and despite its current lively atmosphere the barman spent some time during my visit talking me through its chilling ghostly past.

According to local lore, the pub is haunted by the spirit of a fifteen-year-old girl named Lizzie, from whom it takes its name. Sometime in the eighteenth or nineteenth century, she was kidnapped and forced into prostitution in a makeshift brothel on the building's upper floors.

Tragically, her life was ended when a drunken sailor knocked her unconscious to silence her screams, and when she died shortly afterwards her body was hidden beneath the floorboards.

While I am personally sceptical of such stories, the barman I met was adamant that, over the years, staff and customers have reported eerie phenomena such as sudden cold spots, unexplained noises and even the sensation of cold arms wrapping around them.

One bartender was said to refuse to be alone in the pub after feeling icy hands on his shoulders while alone in the bar.

11. DUNGLOE BAR

Established in 1892, its name comes from the town in neighbouring County Donegal, having become a hub for natives from that rural county who would gather here before taking the 'Derry Boat' to Scotland in search of seasonal work.

Like several of the pubs I visited, it is split into different sections, with a lively music bar, a heated beer garden and the adjoining Harp Bar.

When I filmed here for my socials the barmaid could not stop giggling as I tried to interview her about the pub, which made it even harder for me to understand her accent.

12. PEADAR O'DONNELL'S

Often named as one of Derry's most beloved traditional pubs, it connects internally to its more modern sister bar, the Gweedore, which tends to offer DJs instead of more traditional music.

The building was constructed in the nineteenth century and was the birthplace of Irish revolutionary Liam Devlin in 1877.

After moving to Scotland, Devlin became involved in the Irish Volunteers and, later relocating to Dublin in 1919, he purchased a pub which became the unofficial headquarters for Michael Collins during the War of Independence.

The pub is named after the Donegal-born Irish republican, who lived between 1893 and 1986, and was best known as an IRA commander in the War of Independence and Civil War.

Despite its links to conflict, this lively pub was very welcoming, with a trad band sitting among the customers while I was propped up at the end of the bar with my final Guinness of the crawl.

BOSTON
(**Fenway** to the **Park**)

Few will hear the name Boston without thinking of the famous Red Sox baseball team, so this route starts at their famous ground, before heading along the Back Bay area and on to the edge of Beacon Hill.

Boston is a very walkable city, and although a few roads towards the city centre gave me chills, recalling the steep paths of San Francisco, the wide streets, brownstone buildings and tree-lined avenues feel like stepping into a movie set – which you can literally do, whether braving the queues outside *Cheers* or sitting for a moment of reflection on the Good Will Hunting bench.

I particularly loved the quirky Bukowski Tavern and Anchovies for their friendly character and charm.

Sevens Ale House was the perfect place to end, and the route descended into a bit of chaos thanks to the excitement of game day and the buzz running through the city.

Start from Fenway Park (4 Jersey Street, MA 02215).

1. **Cask 'n Flagon** *1.00 p.m.*
62 Brookline Avenue, MA 02215

2. **Bleacher Bar** *1.30 p.m.*
82A Lansdowne Street, MA 02215

3. **The Lansdowne (open from 4 p.m. weekdays)** *2.15 p.m.*
9 Lansdowne Street, MA 02215

4. **A.T. O'Keeffe's** *3.00 p.m.*
911 Boylston Street, MA 02115

5. **Dillon's** *3.30 p.m.*
955 Boylston Street, MA 02115

6. **Bukowski Tavern** *4.00 p.m.*
50 Dalton Street, MA 02115

7. **Anchovies** *4.45 p.m.*
433 Columbus Avenue, MA 02116

8. **Clerys (closed Sun/Mon)** *5.30 p.m.*
113 Dartmouth Street, MA 02116

9. **OAK Long Bar & Kitchen** *6.15 p.m.*
138 St James Avenue, MA 02116

10. **M.J. O'Connor's** *7.00 p.m.*
27 Columbus Avenue, MA 02116

11. **Cheers** *8.00 p.m.*
84 Beacon Street, MA 02108

12. **Sevens Ale House** *8.45 p.m.*
77 Charles Street, MA 02114

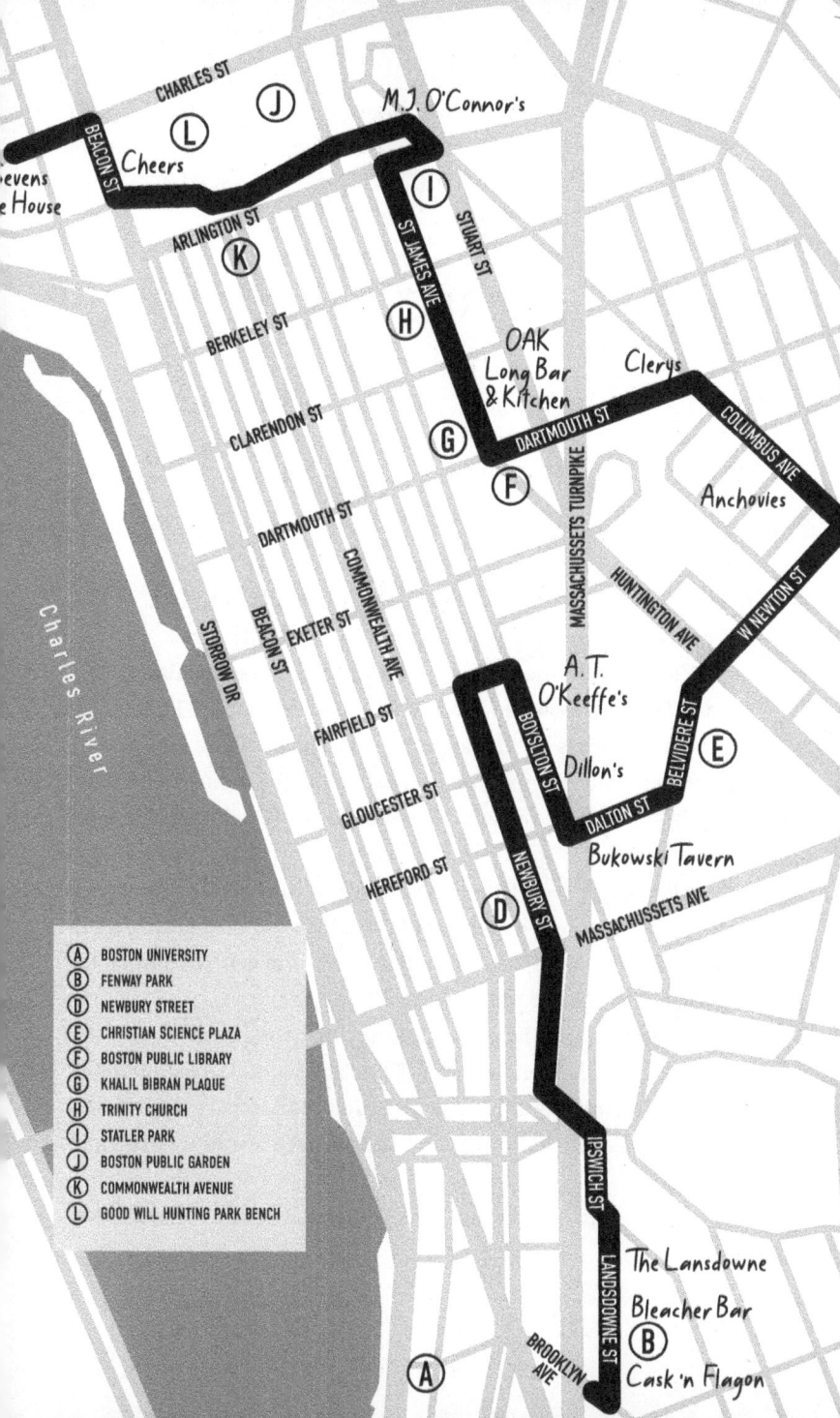

DIRECTIONS

Start around the corner from Boston University **(A)**, where **Cask 'n Flagon (1)** is opposite Fenway Park **(B)**.

Continue by the side of the ground to **Bleacher Bar (2, C)**, with **The Lansdowne (3)** a few yards further along. Follow the road as it curves left through the underpass, before continuing to the end and turning left to reach a major junction. Go diagonally across here, where Newbury Street **(D)** is opposite, one block north.

After a couple of blocks, turn right and then right again at the main road, where **A.T. O'Keeffe's (4)** and **Dillon's (5)** are a few doors apart, with **Bukowski Tavern (6)** opposite, attached to the car park.

Continue past the pub and follow the road as it curves left, with Christian Science Plaza **(E)** on the right. Cross the main road and continue to the next major road, where **Anchovies (7)** is on the left-hand side and **Clerys (8)** a few blocks further along.

Turn right out of the pub and head north, where **OAK**

Long Bar (9) is on the corner opposite the library **(F)**. Turn right past Trinity Church **(G, H)**, where **M.J. O'Connor's (10)** is opposite Statler Park **(I)**.

Head into Boston Public Garden **(J)**, not forgetting to peek down Commonwealth Avenue **(K)** about halfway across the park on the west side, before passing the Good Will Hunting bench **(L)**.

Heading out of the north end of the park, it is easy to spot the famous frontage of **Cheers (11)**, while **Sevens Ale House (12)** is down the second left past the bar.

A. BOSTON UNIVERSITY

Founded in 1839, this prominent institution is one of the largest research universities in the United States. However, it is for its commitment to inclusivity that it is probably best known.

It was one of the first to admit students regardless of race or gender, and in 1872 became the first to award a woman a PhD, when Helen Magill White achieved the honour for her study of Greek.

Another notable doctorate is that awarded to Martin Luther King Jr, who earned his PhD in systematic theology in 1955.

The university's official colour, scarlet, is the reason its Boston terrier mascot is named Rhett, after the leading male character in the 1939 film *Gone with the Wind* – since no one loves Scarlett more than Rhett.

1. CASK 'N FLAGON

Opened initially as a small neighbourhood bar in 1969 it has since become a major part of the Fenway baseball experience.

Housed in what was once a Ford car dealership, the original terrazzo flooring remains, and the back bar uses one of the establishment's early names, Oliver's, for its nightclub and music venue, which has hosted the likes of Bruce Springsteen, Jimi Hendrix and local band Boston.

I was not expecting there to be a game on when I visited to film, so you can imagine the chaos that ensued as 37,000 fans descended on the area several hours in advance to start the all-day drinking session early.

Voted among the top 10 US sports bars, the atmosphere here is electric on game day.

B. FENWAY PARK

Having opened in 1912, it is the oldest Major League Baseball stadium still in use, with a capacity of more than 37,000.

Considered one of the most iconic sports venues in the United States, its construction was part of a wave of steel-and-concrete stadiums built in the early twentieth century, to replace the older wooden structures.

One of Fenway's most recognisable features is a 37-foot-high left-field wall, nicknamed 'the green monster'. Because the wall is so close to home plate – just 310 feet away – its height was designed to keep balls from flying out of the stadium too easily, frustrating right-handed hitters chasing home runs.

Despite efforts to relocate or replace the ageing stadium, public resistance and the deep emotional connection fans have to the ballpark have kept it in place.

2. BLEACHER BAR

Located beneath the centre-field bleachers (which is the raised seating that the rest of the world would call terraces) of Fenway Park, it was originally used as the visiting team's indoor batting cage, until it was converted into a bar in 2008, giving it the distinctive feature of a garage-door-style retractable window that opens onto the centre field, meaning you can view the game without buying a ticket.

There is a similar view from the men's toilets, where two-way glass above the urinals provides a surprising view of the field. This was the result of a mistake during construction but was ultimately embraced as a novelty.

One of the best views in Boston, looking out over the famous Fenway Park, with a beer in hand.

C. RED SOX

One of baseball's most celebrated teams (or as the US audience would say, 'franchises'), it was founded in 1901 as one of the Major League's original eight teams and officially known as the Boston Americans.

Since the team played in red sports stockings, the name Red Sox was adopted in 1908, and they quickly established themselves as one of the most dominant teams in early baseball history.

After winning the first World Series (named more for the fact that it was promoted by the *New York World* newspaper than the idea that eight teams in a single country represented a global competition) the Red Sox went on to capture five more championships over the next two decades, led by the likes of the legendary Babe Ruth.

After selling Ruth to the New York Yankees – a move that was dubbed 'the curse of the bambino' – the team suffered numerous near-misses, dramatic defeats and heartbreaking losses, leading to a championship drought that lasted eighty-six years, until they overturned a 3–0 series deficit to conquer the New York Yankees in 2004 before proceeding to beat the St Louis Cardinals in the World Series.

3. THE LANSDOWNE

This relatively new, lively bar, which opened in 2009, is a great example of a typical large, US-style Irish pub, with a huge bar, high ceilings and a labyrinth of rooms.

We grabbed some pints in the snug, which – in typical US fashion – was probably bigger on its own than many of the pubs I visited in Ireland for this book.

Lansdowne Street has been an important location for the city's live music scene, with neighbours at number 15 hosting the Boston Tea Party concert, as well as iconic bands like the Who, Led Zeppelin and the Velvet Underground, before the historic nightclubs were demolished and replaced by the House of the Blues, which opened around the same time as the pub.

The beauty of researching these routes is that I wasn't expecting to visit here, but its floral frontage and lively atmosphere led to a change of plans and the day's camera assistant, Sarah, grabbing her first pint.

D. NEWBURY STREET

This mile-long, tree-lined boulevard was originally part of a vast tidal marshland before a reclamation project during the 1860s.

The first building constructed on the street was Emmanuel Church in 1861, but as commercial demand increased over time the lower blocks transformed into stores and restaurants.

Today, following the influx of high-end fashion brands, luxury stores and art galleries, it is one of the most expensive retail streets in the US.

As I visited on a Sunday, the road was closed and filled with market stalls and food outlets, with cornhole being played in the street.

4. A.T. O'KEEFFE'S

The self-proclaimed oldest sports bar in America, although let's not let the truth get in the way of a good story as its title is mainly due to its occupancy of the former 'McGreevy's' venue, which was home to Michael 'Nuf Ced' McGreevy's Third Base Saloon from the late 1800s.

5. DILLON'S

Housed in a historic building that was originally built in 1887 and once served as Boston Police Department's Division 16 station, it gets its name from Captain S. Dillon, who was stationed here between 1920 and 1950.

Over the years, Dillon's evolved into a neighbourhood gathering spot, before becoming the bar it is known as today.

Downstairs the cells have vanished and, ironically, made way for an elegant speakeasy.

6. BUKOWSKI TAVERN

Often simply called 'The Buk', it opened in 1998 and is named after poet and writer Charles Bukowski, who was nicknamed the 'laureate of American lowlife'. Owners Kurt and Suzi have been running the place together for the last twenty-eight years.

The notorious dive bar features the Dead Authors Club, where regulars who have tried one hundred different beers earn a mug decorated with an image of their favourite deceased author.

On Boston Marathon days it is a popular spot, given its

location between the finish line and Fenway Park.

The bar also features a 'wheel of fortune' to help you choose what to order, featuring everything from 'safe IPAs' and 'the bartender's choice' to sours and shots.

E. CHRISTIAN SCIENCE PLAZA

Not to be confused with Scientology, which was founded by sci-fi writer L. Ron Hubbard, Christian Science is based on the teachings of the Bible.

This complex, which spans approximately 13.5 acres, was built around the Mother Church of Christ in 1894, with the domed extension added in 1906.

The plaza was redesigned around the 1960s into a modernist public space, with the inclusion of Brutalist-style structures such as the Administration Building and the Church Colonnade. It is the city's largest privately owned public space.

The plaza is home to the Mapparium, whose globe is one of Boston's most photographed tourist attractions – not only for its colourful historical mapping but also for its surreal acoustics, which allow whispered messages to travel right across the dome.

7. ANCHOVIES

This tiny, eclectic bar was one of those most mentioned by my followers before my trip to research this route, and the queer-friendly local is usually packed out.

Staff have a liberal policy when it comes to customers etching designs onto the furniture, and will turn a blind eye if it is not done obviously.

Among the bar's specials is a martini that is doubled up and served along with the shaker so you get two-for-one.

The switch to cocktails mid-route was a bold choice and the day's assistant, Sarah, couldn't resist trying it.

8. CLERYS

Ask the locals how to pronounce this, as it is often mistaken as 'Cleary's'. It was named after the famous Dublin clock and department store.

The unusual resin floor downstairs is usually hard to see, as the venue is open until the small hours for late-night drinks and dancing.

9. OAK LONG BAR

Located inside the historic Fairmont Copley Plaza hotel, which opened in 1912. The hotel was designed by Henry Janeway Hardenbergh and intended to be Boston's most luxurious.

The bar area originally served as a formal dining room known as the Oak Room due its ornate woodwork, high ceilings and old-world charm.

It earned a lively reputation by hosting Boston's elite during Prohibition, and part of the original circular bar rail remains visible in the floor.

Famous for its cocktails, the day's filming went downhill from here on, as the team were keen to offer us a variety of their specialist cocktails and after sampling several we had to tear ourselves away from the bar – because we can't be stopping when we've got to crawl!

F. BOSTON PUBLIC LIBRARY

Founded in 1848, it was the first large free municipal library in the United States and established a model that many American public libraries would later follow – offering things we might take for granted today, like free access to books, public reading rooms, branch locations and a dedicated children's department.

The library is composed of two major buildings, with the original McKim Building opening in 1895 and considered an architectural masterpiece, as its grand marble staircase, vaulted ceilings and intricate mural are inspired by Renaissance libraries in Europe.

The Johnson Building was added in 1972, designed by architect Philip Johnson, famous for Pittsburgh's cathedral-like PPG Place skyscraper.

One of the largest collections in the United States, the library holds more than 23 million items, including medieval manuscripts, early American maps and first editions.

G. KHALIL GIBRAN PLAQUE

Installed to honour the prolific Lebanese-American poet and philosopher Khalil Gibran, most famous for his guide to living, in the book *The Prophet*.

Gibran spent his formative years in Boston after arriving as a teenager in the 1890s. While living with his family in the South End, he taught himself English and immersed himself in the city's intellectual life.

Overlooking the library, its modest presence represents Gibran's humility and legacy as an immigrant's gratitude immortalised in bronze, nestled at the heart of the city that helped shape his beginnings.

H. TRINITY CHURCH

Serving an Episcopal congregation from 1733, it became the main place of worship following the Great Fire of 1872 that engulfed the two older churches.

Construction of the current building took place between 1872 and 1877, with its bold interpretation of Romanesque design becoming an immediate sensation – in an architectural poll of 1885 it was voted the finest building in the United States. In fact, it is now the only survivor of that original top-ten list.

Its striking interior is renowned for its 'vivid polychrome' decoration by painter John La Farge, including expansive murals and stained-glass windows. The free-standing altar was positioned to encourage communal worship, which was a departure from the more traditional Anglican layouts of the time.

10. M.J. O'CONNOR'S

Opened at the turn of the century by Oisin, the pub is still run by the family and anywhere would struggle to host a more diverse range of folks, from Sir Alex Ferguson to Justin Bieber.

By this point I was feeling the pace from the number of beers and cocktail mixers I'd imbibed, and the next walk through the park in the sun was very much appreciated.

I. STATLER PARK

Easy to miss, this small triangular green space got its name from the neighbouring Statler Hotel, built by hotelier E. M. Statler in the 1920s before being renamed the Boston Park Plaza.

It is hard to imagine now, but before the land reclamation developments of the nineteenth century this would have been part of Boston's shoreline.

J. BOSTON PUBLIC GARDEN

Becoming the first public botanical garden in the United States when it was established in 1837, it covers approximately 24 acres and was built to contrast with the busy city life.

The current layout was installed in 1858, before a suspension bridge was constructed over the lagoon in 1867. It would have originally been tidal marshland until it was filled with soil from nearby Beacon Hill and thousands of trees planted.

Throughout the garden are numerous points of interest, and statues of the likes of George Washington, with the Ether Monument – erected to commemorate the first public display of anaesthesia – the oldest of these, having been unveiled in 1868.

K. COMMONWEALTH AVENUE

With the nickname 'Comm Ave', this grand boulevard runs from Boston Public Garden through Back Bay and into Route 30.

It was originally laid out in the mid-1850s by architect Arthur Gilman under notable park planner Frederick Law Olmsted's guidance, with uniform tree planting by 1888 (yes, that was an actual job responsibility).

Forming part of what is known as Boston's Emerald Necklace park system, it hosts dozens of monuments, including statues of Alexander Hamilton, William Lloyd Garrison, Samuel Eliot Morison and Patrick Collins, and the Boston Women's Memorial honouring former first lady Abigail Adams, leading suffragist Lucy Stone, and African American poet Phillis Wheatley.

Its name was reportedly just a placeholder proposed by Gilman, but it stuck despite other ideas.

L. GOOD WILL HUNTING PARK BENCH

Written by childhood friends Matt Damon and Ben Affleck, the 1997 film *Good Will Hunting* tells the tale of janitor Will Hunting, who is secretly a self-taught mathematical genius.

After the title character assaults a police officer, he is spared jail on the proviso that he studies with one of the university's professors alongside regular sessions with therapist Sean, played by Robin Williams.

Many of the city's landmarks feature throughout the film, with the park bench scene between Will and Sean becoming one of the film's most iconic moments, and it remains a popular spot for fans to visit. The scene was largely unscripted, with much of the emotional dialogue ad-libbed by Williams. His words about the value of experience are a wake-up call to the young prodigy.

It is hard to watch back these days knowing that Robin Williams took his own life some years later. So always make sure to check on your friends and family, because you rarely know what is happening behind the scenes.

The origin of one of the film's most popular lines, 'How do you like them apples?', remains a mystery, with the most likely being linked to World War I slang, where British soldiers would refer to grenades as 'toffee apples'. These days the phrase is typically used to taunt or tease someone after a victory.

11. CHEERS

Founded in 1969 as the Bull & Finch Pub, it earned its status as a global icon when, in 1982, it was chosen by the creators of the NBC sitcom *Cheers* to represent their fictional tavern, with the exterior becoming the memorable establishing shot of the TV show's opening credits.

Despite its fame, it was not until 2002 that the pub officially changed its name to Cheers Beacon Hill after securing a licensing deal with NBC.

Although the interior includes an upstairs replica of the television set, the layout of the bar is unrecognisable from the studio set where filming took place. Despite this, there is a queue outside at almost all times.

Based in the place 'where everybody knows your name', *Cheers* was a classic American television sitcom that originally aired across eleven series from 1982 to 1993 and consisted of 275 episodes.

Episodes revolved around the cosy basement bar and the group of regular staff and patrons. The central characters included Sam Malone, a former Red Sox relief pitcher and recovering alcoholic, played by Ted Danson; Diane Chambers, portrayed by Shelley Long, who was an intellectual waitress with lofty ambitions; Carla Tortelli, the tough-talking waitress played by Rhea Perlman; and a sweet, naive bartender played by Woody Harrelson.

Regulars on the other side of the bar included beer-loving Norm Peterson, who rarely moved from his stool at the end of the bar; Cliff Clavin, who was a wise-cracking, know-it-all mailman; and Kelsey Grammer's psychologist Frasier Crane, who went on to enjoy success in his own show.

Although it struggled in the ratings during its first season, the show quickly built a devoted audience and became a cultural phenomenon that led to critical acclaim and twenty-eight Emmy Awards.

It became one of the most watched television shows of all time, and the series finale, which aired in 1993, drew an audience of nearly 84 million, which is staggering considering that, in those days, there were no watch-on-demand streaming services.

Few sitcom characters are as recognisable as Norm, who propped up this famous bar.

12. SEVENS ALE HOUSE

Known locally as 'The Sevens', this pub has operated continuously since 1933, making it one of Boston's oldest.

Even though Hollywood icon Harrison Ford visited in 2017, this time around they had to make do with a 'legend in his own lunchtime' turning up at the end of a pub crawl.

While I missed the chance to meet owner Jules, who has taken over the bar from her father who purchased it in the mid-1970s, there was a friendly bunch of locals present, and I managed to bump into John who follows my social accounts and had made a special trip into the city.

It was chaos at the end of the route when social media follower John joined for the final pints.

BOSTON
(Revolution to Freedom)

Starting in the harbour at historic Charlestown, this route crosses into the city and roughly follows the Freedom Trail and the many iconic sights along the way.

Featuring some of the oldest pubs, not just in Boston but in the US as a whole, the city feels proud of its Irish revolutionary history throughout.

Walking through the quiet, narrow roads, past the wooden-slatted buildings adorned in American flags, Charlestown felt like a world away from the bustling tourist markets, food stalls selling fresh oysters and street performers around Faneuil Hall.

The route includes a mix of proper dark-wood Irish boozers like Emmets and the Black Rose, while also including storied bars that share tales of JFK, Malcolm X and Ho Chi Minh.

With such a large Irish population, Boston felt like a home away from Ireland, and a worthy location that I was so happy to add to this book.

Start at the Anchor Bar (1 Shipyard Park, MA 02129).

1. **The Anchor** *1.00 p.m.*
1 Shipyard Park, MA 02129

2. **Warren Tavern** *1.45 p.m.*
2 Pleasant Street, MA 02129

3. **Blackmoor Bar & Kitchen** *2.30 p.m.*
1 Chelsea Street, MA 02129

4. **Teddy's On The Hill/The Red Hat** *3.15 p.m.*
9 Bowdoin Street, MA 02114

5. **21st Amendment** *4.00 p.m.*
150 Bowdoin Street, MA 02108

6. **Emmets** *4.45 p.m.*
6 Beacon Street, MA 02108

7. **The Last Hurrah** *5.15 p.m.*
60 School Street, MA 02108

8. **J.J. Foley's Bar & Grille** *6.00 p.m.*
21 Kingston Street, MA 02111

9. **The Black Rose** *7.00 p.m.*
160 State Street, MA 02109

10. **The Green Dragon Tavern** *7.45 p.m.*
11 Marshall Street, MA 02108

11. **The Bell in Hand** *8.30 p.m.*
45 Union Street, MA 02108

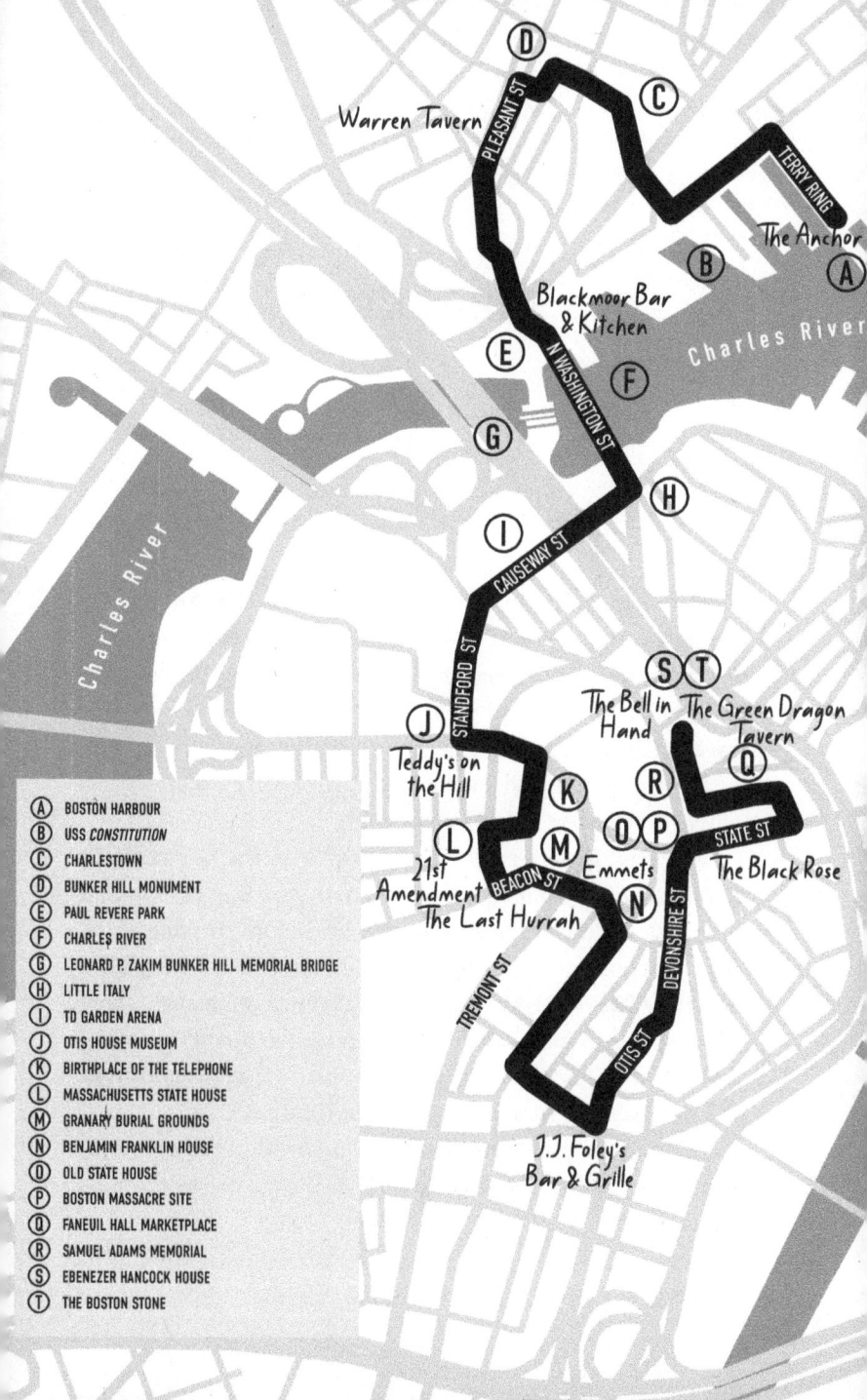

DIRECTIONS

Start overlooking Boston Harbour **(A)** at **The Anchor (1)** before turning right at the USS *Constitution* **(B)**, under the highway towards Charlestown **(C)**, and crossing Bunker Hill Monument **(D)** to head down Pleasant Street, where **Warren Tavern (2)** is on the corner.

Continue along Harvard Street, over City Square Park, where **Blackmoor Bar (3)** is opposite.

Pass Paul Revere Park **(E)** and head over the bridge **(F, G)** before turning right at Little Italy **(H)** past the TD Garden arena **(I)**. Follow as the road curves left before crossing at the next junction by Otis House Museum **(J)**, where **Teddy's On The Hill/The Red Hat (4)** is one block down on the left. There is the option to follow the road around to the Birthplace of the Telephone **(K)** before heading up the hill to **21st Amendment (5)**, opposite the Massachusetts State House **(L)**.

Leaving the pub, **Emmets (6)** is just around the corner to the left, with **The Last Hurrah (7)** on the corner of the next street.

Head along Tremont Street past the Granary Burying Grounds **(M)**, before turning left along the brick path of Winter Street, turning right onto Kingston Street to **J.J. Foley's Bar & Grille (8)**.

Turn left out of the pub and head north, with Benjamin Franklin House **(N)** a few yards down Milk Street, before continuing along and turning right at the Old State House **(O, P)**, where **The Black Rose (9)** is a few yards along on the opposite side of the road.

Turn left out of the pub and walk through Faneuil Hall Marketplace **(Q)**, turning right at the Samuel Adams statue **(R)** along Union Street, where **The Green Dragon Tavern (10, S)** and **The Bell in Hand (11, T)** sit opposite at the end of the route.

A. BOSTON

Founded by settlers from England in 1630, Boston is one of the United States' oldest and most historically significant cities.

Originally located on a small peninsula, which has since been expanded through land reclamation, this has given it its unusual shape and haphazard mix of new and old buildings.

Playing a central role in the American Revolution, it was events such as the Boston Massacre in 1770, the Boston Tea Party in 1773, and the Battles of Lexington and Concord in 1775 that cemented Boston's place in the nation's founding story.

Boston is home to several firsts, being the first US city to have a public park (Boston Common, opened in 1634), public school (Boston Latin School, founded in 1635) and subway system (Tremont Street subway, opened in 1897).

The population of the greater Boston area is approximately 25 per cent Irish, accounting for around the same number of people as live in Dublin and its suburbs.

The influx started around the time of the Great Famine of 1845, which saw overwhelming numbers of Irish people emigrate to what was one of their closest major US ports. While many of those who landed in New York went on to move elsewhere, Boston's existing small Irish community, which already practised the same religion and spoke the same language as the newcomers, coupled with the demand for construction, dock and factory workers, meant that many chose to settle here.

By the late nineteenth century, the community was numerous enough to gain political power through the elevation of Irish-American politicians such as the Kennedy family.

1. THE ANCHOR

Opened in 2019, it transformed a former Charlestown Navy Yard industrial structure into a dynamic public gathering space, complete with open-air wine and beer garden, arts programming venue, and waterfront events hub, with views across the harbour.

The naturally deep and sheltered waters of the harbour led to its rise as a key hub for transatlantic trade, fishing and shipbuilding, and the growth of the city as a major global port.

At the edge of the quay is the *Arms of Friendship*, which is the world's largest bronze octopus sculpture, spanning about 36 feet and weighing almost seven tons.

The octopus, which sits surrounded by sculptures of other wild animals, was created by internationally acclaimed artists Gillie and Marc as part of their Wildlife Wonders exhibition. Visitors are invited to climb onto the structure to sit on its giant tentacles among the endangered species. The exhibit is expected to remain in place until the late summer of 2027.

Any chance I can get for a self-congratulatory photo opportunity in this iconic city.

B. USS *CONSTITUTION*

The oldest commissioned warship in the world that remains afloat, it was launched in 1797 as one of the six founding frigates of the United States Navy.

Its nickname, 'Old Ironsides', comes from the ship's battle with British frigates in 1812, when cannonballs from HMS *Guerriere* were seen to bounce off the *Constitution*'s thick oak hull.

With an arsenal of forty-four guns, the ship would have

been manned by a crew of around 450, and although initially a demonstration of naval power and protection for merchant ships against pirates, its later years were spent on goodwill missions, such as its circumnavigation of the globe in the nineteenth century.

Although it was rumoured in the 1830s that there were plans to scrap the ship, the subsequent national outrage, fuelled by Oliver Wendell Holmes's poem, helped save it.

C. CHARLESTOWN

Founded in 1628 – two years before the city – Boston's oldest neighbourhood was originally a separate city before it was annexed in 1874.

It played a crucial part in the American Revolutionary War and built up a large community of Irish immigrants in the nineteenth century.

When I walked up here it felt like stepping back in time, with the wood-clad buildings draped in folded flags and looking like the sort of homes someone with a musket would step out of at any moment.

D. BUNKER HILL MONUMENT

Erected on the site of the battle that took place here between 1825 and 1843, it is accessible via the 294 steps to the top.

The Battle of Bunker Hill was one of the first significant conflicts in the American Revolutionary War, as locals aimed to prevent British troops from fortifying the area first.

It is here that the famous phrase 'Don't fire until you see the whites of their eyes' was said to have been uttered by Colonel

William Prescott – although this has since been debunked, as the phrase was widely used as far back as the 1740s.

Despite its name, the monument is sited on Breed's Hill, where most of the fighting took place, with Bunker Hill the intended site for the fortifications.

2. WARREN TAVERN

Established in 1780, just a few years after the start of the American Revolution, it is named in honour of Dr Joseph Warren, a physician and patriot who was killed at the Battle of Bunker Hill.

One of the country's oldest remaining bars, its history goes back to a time when it was a popular meeting spot for Revolutionary War figures and early American leaders such as Paul Revere and George Washington.

Although it was closed briefly prior to its restoration and reopening in the 1970s, many of its original features – such as exposed wooden beams, old fireplaces and uneven flooring – remain.

Some staff and customers have reported ghostly sightings such as flickering lights, mysterious footsteps and sudden chills.

3. BLACKMOOR BAR

Located opposite the City Square Park, which was where Charlestown was founded in 1628. The park was completely redesigned in the late 1980s as part of the 'Big Dig' project, when all the main roads were moved into tunnels under the city.

But back to the bar . . . It features an outdoor patio area overlooking the harbour and inbound ships.

E. PAUL REVERE PARK

Established in 1999, the park occupies a reclaimed parcel of land that previously served as rail yards and parts of the Central Artery highway structure.

It honours Revolutionary War patriot Paul Revere, who is best known for his midnight ride to warn the local militia of the approach of British troops.

Born in 1734 to a French Huguenot father and Bostonian mother, he worked as an engraver and silversmith, and ran a successful foundry that was important to the city's growth.

F. CHARLES RIVER

Stretching for approximately 80 miles through New England, the river passes twenty-three cities and towns.

It would have been used for fishing by Indigenous Americans, with its Algonquian name being *Quinobequin*, meaning 'meandering'. Following the arrival of European settlers it was renamed in honour of King Charles I.

Unfortunately, by the mid-twentieth century the river had become notorious for its pollution, but efforts to restore it did not begin in earnest until the 1960s when it appeared in the lyrics of 'Dirty Water', a song by LA garage-rock band the Standells.

G. LEONARD P. ZAKIM BUNKER HILL MEMORIAL BRIDGE

A striking feature of the Boston skyline, it was completed in 2003 as part of the 'Big Dig' project to replace Boston's elevated highway with an underground tunnel system.

The bridge is named in honour of both the civil rights activist and director of the New England Anti-Defamation League, and the Battle of Bunker Hill, which took place nearby.

At 1,432 feet long, it was the widest cable-stayed bridge in the world at the time of its completion, and remains one of the most technically ambitious bridges in the country due to its two inverted Y-shaped towers, intended to represent a 'balance' of past and present.

H. LITTLE ITALY

The city's oldest residential neighbourhood, it was first settled by English colonists in the 1600s, but by the late nineteenth and early twentieth centuries, had transformed into a bustling hub for Italian immigrants.

The area is a mix of important historic sites, such as Paul Revere House, and iconic eateries like Mike's Pastry and Modern Pastry.

Also in the district is the famous Old North Church, where the sexton lit lanterns, 'one if by land, two if by sea', to warn of the approach of British troops, as part of the alert system used on the night of Paul Revere's midnight ride.

I. TD GARDEN ARENA

Opened in 1995 to replace the original Boston Garden, which was built in 1928 by the boxing promoter behind Madison Square Garden.

The arena hosts the Boston Bruins ice hockey team, which is one of the 'original six' and the oldest in the United States. Playing in black, white and yellow, the Bruins have won the Stanley Cup six times, which makes them equal fourth with the Chicago Blackhawks in terms of most wins, behind the Montreal Canadiens, the Toronto Maple Leafs and the Detroit Red Wings.

The famous Boston Celtics basketball team also plays here, with its eighteen NBA championships making this league-founding member the most successful in history. It also holds a winning record over every NBA team apart from the San Antonio Spurs.

The Celtics' rise to dominance began in the 1950s, with further glory years in the mid-1970s and 1980s, when 'The Hick from French Lick', Larry Bird, anchored the team before he went on to a Hall of Fame career that has seen him regarded as one of the greatest players of all time.

J. OTIS HOUSE MUSEUM

The first of three mansions designed by renowned architect Charles Bulfinch for statesman Harrison Gray Otis, it was constructed in 1795 and is a rare surviving example of the elegant residences that once dominated this area.

Otis was one the most influential early Americans, serving as a congressman and mayor, as well as developing a huge portfolio of real estate.

The family lived in the house for only a few years, until about 1801, after which it served as a clinic, a boarding house and then eventually office space.

It survived demolition in the mid-twentieth century, more by luck than anything else, with its position – set back from the main street, following restoration efforts and relocation in 1920 – saving it from developers.

4. TEDDY'S ON THE HILL/THE RED HAT

The original Red Hat bar opened in 1907, making it one of the city's oldest, and continued as a speakeasy for local sailors and travellers throughout Prohibition.

After closing in mid-2021 due to an ownership change and the struggles during the pandemic, it was revived and reopened early the following year with a new name, Teddy's On The Hill.

K. BIRTHPLACE OF THE TELEPHONE

It was from the top floor of a boarding house in Exeter Street, on 10 March 1876, that Alexander Graham Bell called his assistant over a telephone line, 'Mr Watson, come here. I want to see you.'

Legend has it that the phrase was not chosen for some dramatic meaning but more out of necessity, as Bell had spilled acid on his prototype during an experiment.

The invention came about as a result of Bell's experiments while teaching at Boston University, and his work on the harmonic telegraph, intended to assist the deaf community. These efforts resulted in the combination of wire coils, magnets and membranes that would form the basis of voice communication for over a century, until digital methods were developed.

Bell managed to file the patent for his invention on Valentine's Day 1876, just hours before a rival inventor, Elisha Gray, who many claim pioneered the liquid transmitter several years before Bell, was alleged to have stolen the idea from him.

Although the building where this historic moment took place no longer exists, its location is marked both by a plaque and an engraving on the sidewalk.

5. 21ST AMENDMENT

Named after the 1933 change in the US Constitution that repealed the eighteenth amendment and ended the period of Prohibition that had banned the manufacture and sale of alcohol nationwide from 1920.

It is the only amendment that repeals another amendment, as well as being the only one ratified by state conventions rather than state legislators, to both speed up the process and circumvent political disruption.

As this location previously housed a men's political club, there may have been additional incentives and encouragement to bypass the red tape and political motives.

And where there is a bar there is a beer, so I grabbed a pint and sat at the table where JFK himself was said to have sat and worked.

Said to be the table where JFK sat to write, and here I was tallying up the day's pints.

L. MASSACHUSETTS STATE HOUSE

Overlooking Boston Common, this iconic Beacon Hill building was completed in 1798 and designed by Charles Bulfinch, one of America's first professional architects.

Its distinctive golden dome was gilded in 1874, but was temporarily painted over during World War II to avoid glare during air raids.

The land on which it is built was originally a cow pasture belonging to John Hancock, who was the first Governor of Massachusetts, with the cornerstone laid in 1795 at a ceremony that included Samuel Adams and Paul Revere.

6. EMMETS

Named after the Irish revolutionary who was born in 1778 and celebrated for his defiant speech, which included the lines 'Let no man write my epitaph . . . until my country takes her place among the nations of the earth', as he was tried for high treason.

Romanticised as a national hero by Irish communities across the United States, with statues in Washington, DC, San Francisco and Boston, he met a gruesome end when he was hanged and beheaded at the age of just twenty-five outside St Catherine's Church in Dublin.

These days, the bar claims to have Boston's best Irish coffee, which was unfortunate for local Sarah, who joined me to film the route, as it was her first ever taste of one, so it was all downhill from there!

7. THE LAST HURRAH

This bar is nestled on the ground floor of the Omni Parker House hotel, which was founded in 1855 and hosted the likes of Charles Dickens, Ralph Waldo Emerson and abolitionist Amos Bronson Alcott.

John Wilkes Booth was seen practising at a nearby firing range during a visit to his actor brother, eight days before he assassinated Abraham Lincoln in 1865.

Other notable figures and events claimed to have been associated with the hotel include John F. Kennedy proposing to Jacqueline Bouvier, and Ho Chi Minh and Malcolm X, both of whom were rumoured to have worked at the hotel.

M. GRANARY BURYING GROUNDS

Boston's third-oldest cemetery was established in 1660 and took its name from the granary building that once stood nearby.

Among the five thousand individuals laid to rest at the two-acre site are colonial rights activist James Otis, Benjamin Franklin's parents, Josiah and Abiah, the three signatories of the Declaration of Independence: John Hancock, Samuel Adams and Robert Treat Paine, and Boston icon Paul Revere.

Near the centre of the cemetery is a shared headstone for the victims of the 1770 Boston Massacre.

Unfounded speculation suggests that Mary, the wife of Isaac Goose, was the inspiration for Mother Goose, the imaginary author of a collection of French fairy tales. Her grave here is the only reliable reminder of this as, despite tales of the songs she sung to her grandchildren, and their subsequent printing and distribution, no trace of them has been found, with historians believing the whole story was concocted by the great-grandson of her son-in-law.

8. J.J. FOLEY'S BAR & GRILLE

Not to be confused with the city's oldest continuously operating Irish pub, established in 1909 by Jeremiah Foley, and named by social media Guinness expert Jason Hackett, aka PrimeMutton, as one of the United States' best pints.

Unfortunately, that pub is a lot further out of town, so for the purpose of a walkable route I've included this one instead, which still offers a cracking pint and is run by the same family.

N. BENJAMIN FRANKLIN HOUSE

One of the founding fathers of the United States, Benjamin Franklin was born on 17 January 1706 on Milk Street, at the heart of Boston's financial district.

Although the original building was destroyed by fire in 1811, its location is marked by a plaque on the street.

Despite this acknowledgement, some historians have

debated whether Franklin was in fact born in nearby Hanover Street, based on descriptions of his father's soap and candle shop.

However, let us not let the truth get in the way of a good story when we've got pubs to go to.

O. OLD STATE HOUSE

Built in 1713 on the site of Boston's original Town House, it is the city's oldest surviving public building, and would have housed the Massachusetts General Court, the Royal Governors, and various other administrative and judicial organisations.

It was here, in 1761, inside the Council Chamber, that James Otis Jr delivered his famous speech against the 'Writs of Assistance'. These were essentially general search warrants, and so this became an early spark of resistance to British rule. Just nine years later, in 1770, the Boston Massacre took place on its doorstep, marking one of the first incidents of bloodshed in colonial unrest.

On 18 July 1776, the Declaration of Independence was proclaimed from the building's east balcony, as Colonel Thomas Crafts read it out to the cheering crowds that had gathered below. Following this, symbols of British rule, such as lion and unicorn statues, were removed and destroyed.

After independence, the building served as the seat of Massachusetts' state government, and from 1830 to 1841 it was Boston's City Hall.

By the mid-nineteenth century, it was increasingly being used for commercial purposes, before campaigners rescued it and converted it into a museum celebrating Boston's revolutionary heritage.

P. BOSTON MASSACRE SITE

Taking place on the steps of the Old State House on the evening of 5 March 1770, one of the most pivotal moments in the build-up to the American Revolution occurred when British soldiers fired into a crowd, killing five men and wounding many more.

The incident began when a group of colonists confronted a solitary British sentry stationed outside the Custom House.

As more civilians gathered, they began shouting insults and throwing snowballs, ice and debris at the soldiers who had arrived to support the guard.

The tension escalated into chaos when it is believed someone shouted 'fire', leading to the British forces shooting into the crowd, first killing Crispus Attucks, who is often referred to as the first American killed in the revolution.

The next day the soldiers were arrested and tried for murder, with future president John Adams defending them in court, resulting in the acquittal of six and the final two receiving what seems like a rather trivial branding of the thumb to acknowledge their manslaughter conviction.

Three years later, on the night of 16 December 1773, protests against the Tea Act, which bypassed the trade of colonial merchants, led to demonstrators disguised as Indigenous Americans boarding three docked ships – the *Dartmouth*, *Eleanor* and *Beaver* – before dumping 342 chests of tea, worth around £10,000 (equivalent to US$2.5 million in 2025), in the harbour.

The ruling government closed the harbour and passed a series of Coercive Acts – known by patriots as Intolerable Acts – that caused outrage and pushed the colonies closer to armed resistance.

9. THE BLACK ROSE

Opened in 1976, the pub gets its name from the Gaelic poem 'Róisín Dubh', which means 'little black rose'.

It was another pub that was highly requested ahead of my trip, and it was a great to bump into local Matthew, who follows my socials and joined us for the last few pubs.

One of the real joys of researching these books is when I get to share them with fellow pub enthusiasts and swap notes over a beer.

Q. FANEUIL HALL

One of the most iconic and historically significant buildings in Boston, and perhaps the US, with the nickname 'The Cradle of Liberty'.

It has served as the city's main public meeting hall and marketplace since it was built in 1742, its name honouring the wealthy merchant Peter Faneuil, who funded the development.

It is an iconic location, the site of many passionate speeches in the lead-up to the American Revolution, as Samuel Adams,

James Otis and Dr Joseph Warren fought against taxation, tax-related acts and the fallout from the Boston Massacre.

The building was expanded to a third floor in 1806, by Charles Bulfinch, widely considered the first American-born professional architect.

On top of the building sits a weathervane in the shape of a grasshopper. It was crafted in 1742 by Sheffield-born Deacon Shem Drowne, who had the honour of being Boston's first recorded weathervane maker. Measuring around 4 feet long, it is likely to have been a nod to the one on London's Royal Exchange.

Legend has it that to identify outsiders, locals would ask suspected spies about the 'grasshopper on the market', with those unfamiliar with it being questioned further.

R. SAMUEL ADAMS MEMORIAL

Sculptured by pioneering female artist Anne Whitney, this prominent statue was erected in 1880 and depicts the revolutionary powerhouse standing defiantly with his arms folded and dressed in colonial attire.

Adams was – with John Hancock – one of the founders of the Sons of Liberty, a political organisation established to fight unfair taxation of residents.

The statue was originally placed in Adams Square, which was named in his honour, but was later moved to accommodate development of the Government Center buildings.

The paved plaza where the statue now resides features etched lines and motifs indicating the old 1630 shoreline and historic street layout.

10. THE GREEN DRAGON TAVERN

Sometimes referred to as the 'Headquarters of the Revolution', the original pub was built in the late seventeenth century, and became famous as a gathering place for notable patriots Samuel Adams, John Hancock, Paul Revere, Benjamin Franklin and others.

Legend says that it hosted meetings of the Sons of Liberty, and was the launch point for the Boston Tea Party and Paul Revere's midnight ride.

Although the iconic building was demolished in the early nineteenth century, it was rebuilt in 1976 near its original location.

S. EBENEZER HANCOCK HOUSE

Constructed by founding father John Hancock, this rare surviving home was built in 1767 before he transferred ownership to his brother Ebenezer who was the Paymaster General of the Continental Army.

It served as a vital administrative centre during the Revolutionary War, with troops paid from the reportedly two million silver crowns – on loan from France – that were stored here.

When the war ended, it changed hands and by 1798 had become a shoe store that went on to be Boston's longest-running (no pun intended) shoe business until 1963.

11. THE BELL IN HAND

Founded in 1795, it is widely regarded as America's oldest continuously operating tavern, having been opened by Jimmy Wilson, who was the city's last town crier, with the literal bell that he carried being the inspiration for the pub's name.

While the current building is modern, it occupies the site of the original eighteenth-century tavern in one of the oldest areas of the city.

It was rumoured to be a meeting point for early Boston leaders, but today's drinkers are more likely to sense the ghost of the original founder, which is said to haunt the bar.

T. THE BOSTON STONE

Embedded in the base of a brick building on Marshall Street, this mysterious granite sphere is approximately 2 feet across and was imported from England around 1700 by early settler Thomas Childs.

It was used to crush pigments in what was then the town's first paint mill, before it ceased trading and the stone lay discarded until it was incorporated in the new building in the 1730s.

It was not until 1837 that, inspired by the famous London Stone, it received its current moniker, with the inscription turning what was largely forgotten into a minor tourist landmark.

PICTURE CREDITS

Page 57 © Robert Linsdell / Wikimedia Commons
Page 67 © Oliver Dixon / Wikimedia Commons
Page 137 © Nmwalsh / Wikimedia Commons
Page 173 © Tom Parnell / Wikimedia Commons
Page 180 © Albert Bridge / Wikimedia Commons
Page 193 © Keith Ruffles / Wikimedia Commons
Page 196 © N Chadwick / Wikimedia Commons
Page 200 © N Chadwick / Wikimedia Commons

ACKNOWLEDGEMENTS

This book would not exist without the wonderful support of friends, family and, of course, all the great pubs and staff who are there to make these memories.

I am very appreciative of everyone who has followed me on social media and given me the confidence to create further books. The most rewarding times have been when I have seen people in pubs holding one of my books.

This is the first of my books to have been entirely researched and written without any prior experience of the towns and cities that feature. Not only am I very grateful for the fantastic pub selections that have been recommended on social media, I have also had such great times with Luke, Chloe, Lauren, Caden and Sarah, who walked the steps with me and often shared the pints.

Communities have been built around public houses for hundreds of years and it feels like this is never more obvious than in Ireland.

Today, in the modern world, pubs are perfect places to chat, cry or laugh with family and friends.

It has been incredibly hard to compile this book, in the knowledge that so many great pubs and locations will be missed out.

Ireland, I adore you, so I look forward to leaving enough room for the sequel.

Thanks go, of course, to my loving family, exceptional friends and my two hero boys, who make getting up the following day, with a hangover, worthwhile.

Special thanks to the two best guides I could ask for to help me check my routes around Ireland, Daragh Curran and Cassie Stokes.

HOW TO GET INVOLVED

Since publishing my first book of pub crawls in autumn 2023, I have launched Historic Pub Crawls across social media, using the handle @historicpubcrawls, and begun to revisit all the pubs featured in my books.

It is great to meet and spend time with the landlords and staff, rediscover some of the areas, continually improve the details in these books and sample exciting new beers.

The best part about sharing the journey on social media has been receiving suggestions for new routes and pubs to explore.

If you are not already following me then please do, and join in, on the platforms below, as I love to hear about pubs I've missed or should be going to next as we explore more of the country – and the world – in the future.

Find me on TikTok, Instagram and YouTube: @historicpubcrawls.

ABOUT THE AUTHOR

Thomas has been running a pub crawl for his birthday almost every year since his mid-twenties.

After years working in technology, and following the closure of his startup, he decided to compile the years of fun into a handy guide that could be shared with others.

With his debut self-published book in hand, he walked into the first pub and asked for a free pint to film for his social media accounts, before a quick rejection left him slinking off without footage or a pint.

Fast-forward twelve months, and he had gained 250,000 followers, regular slots on national and local radio, and appearances on ITV and the BBC, he is a passionate champion of the community spirit that pubs bring to the heart of towns and cities across the UK.

When he is not writing or in the pub, he plays guitar and piano, and likes tattoos, crazy trousers and yellow shoes.

He lives in north-west London with his two sons.